THE · WORLD · OF
WEDDINGS

THE · WORLD · OF
WEDDINGS
AN ILLUSTRATED CELEBRATION

BRIAN MURPHY

**PADDINGTON
PRESS LTD**
NEW YORK & LONDON

Library of Congress Cataloging in Publication Data

Murphy, Brian Michael.
    The world of weddings.

    1.   Weddings.   2.   Marriage customs and rites.
I.   Title.
GT2665.M87   392'.5   77-21012
ISBN 0-448-22679-0

Filmset and printed in England by BAS Printers Limited, Over Wallop, Hampshire
Bound in England by R. J. Acford Ltd., Chichester, Sussex
Color separations by Rowley Studios Ltd., Hull
Color sections printed by Shenval Press, Harlow, Essex

Designed by Colin Lewis
Picture research by Enid Moore and Kati Boland

In the United States
PADDINGTON PRESS
Distributed by
GROSSET & DUNLAP

In the United Kingdom
PADDINGTON PRESS

In Canada
Distributed by
RANDOM HOUSE OF CANADA LTD.

In Southern Africa
Distributed by
ERNEST STANTON (PUBLISHERS) (PTY.) LTD.

CONTENTS

*A wedding is always an occasion for excitement,
accompanied by gaiety, laughter, perhaps a few
momentary fears and almost certainly one or two tears.
It is one of the most momentous undertakings that either
party will ever make, and one of the most memorable.
However long ago their wedding, few couples cannot
remember what they wore, who attended, who got drunk,
what the weather was like and details of the ceremony
and celebration. But what bride and groom may forget in
their personal excitement is that they are participating in
a ritual which goes back beyond our oldest surviving
religions and exists, in its various forms, throughout the
world.*

*They might be surprised to discover how many of the
customs they observe would be familiar to young couples
in the ancient world: the Roman bridegroom also carried
his bride over the threshold of their new home; our rice
and confetti echo the Greek practice of throwing nuts and
fruit; and the Israelites would be happy to learn that the
blue ribbon worn by their bride—a symbol of purity, love
and fidelity—has survived as "something blue." And so
it is throughout the world of weddings: cakes, rings,
veils, feasts, ceremonies, traditions—all have their
counterparts in other times, other cultures. The wedding
ceremony is the universally traditional overture to the
establishment of a family, the fundamental building
block of society.*

*This remains as true today as it was when our primitive
ancestors entered into the first formal pact to guarantee
companionship for each other and security and a home for
their future children. Indeed, despite attacks on the
institutions of marriage and the family, despite the
phenomena of "living together" and rising divorce rates,
most young people continue to regard marriage as the
ideal circumstance in which to seek a fulfilled
and happy life.*

*All species reproduce, and many are monogamous. But
only humanity, fired by its unique imagination and sense
of mystery, has invented the wedding ceremony, the rite of
passage which affirms the sanctity of wedlock and the
belief that:*

Our state cannot be sever'd; we are one,
One flesh; to lose thee were to lose myself.

John Milton wrote these words in Paradise Lost *over
three hundred years ago; they still hold good for many
people. To them, and to those who cherish memories of
their own wedding, or who look forward to one in the
future; to those who are curious to know how our modern
wedding developed, or how it is celebrated elsewhere, this
book is dedicated.*

A WEDDING HAS BEEN ARRANGED — WHY?

"The first bond of society is marriage" CICERO

IT IS A startling fact that, regardless of geography, religion, social customs or political systems, weddings everywhere have always shared certain characteristics. The bride may be specially dressed, anointed and coiffed, and may be veiled or crowned. There may be a special feast for friends and relations, at which she will sit beside the groom at a selected spot. The occasion will be marked by gifts. When she reaches her new home, there may be some ceremony at the entrance to mark her crossing the threshold, denoting her passage not only from her father's care to her new husband's, but also from childhood in her previous family to adulthood at the beginning of a new one. The couple may be addressed by some person respected in the community who will speak of past virtues and hope for happiness and children to come. There may also be some ritual such as the scattering of rice, nuts, flower petals or fruit to evoke, by sympathetic magic, the blessing of children upon the couple. The bride may express sorrow at leaving her parents, the parents may shed a tear at the "loss" of their son or daughter, the parents of the groom may make his bride publicly welcome and promise to look after her. The ceremony may take place before members of the bride's or groom's community.

Ceremonial behavior of this kind is reported in the earliest accounts of the ancient Greeks and Romans, of the Jews from the time of Abraham, and of the Medes and Persians. It has continued down the years to survive the French, Russian and Chinese revolutions, and the rise and fall of religions.

So it would appear that "a wedding has been arranged" because we feel a deep-seated urge that it should be. This urge is partly practical, partly mystical, but it is surprising how small a part religion and the modern concept of romantic love have played in the wedding ceremony. Many ceremonies have a religious aspect, but by no means all: some have legal, financial and social aspects only.

8

One of the world's leading religions, Islam, has no specific religious ceremony of marriage. The early Christians did not regard marriage as a religious matter, and it was not until A.D. 537 that it was decided that marriage among the leaders of the community should be made a religious ceremony. The peasants were, as so often, allowed to get on with things as they wished for many years to come. It was not until the Council of Trent in 1563 that a religious ceremony was made an essential part of a lawful Catholic marriage. England moved more slowly still and did not pass similar legislation until 1753. This only lasted until 1836 when the Registration Act restored the right of English couples to conclude a secular marriage. By contrast, the United States has always had a tradition of secular marriage, ever since the arrival of the first Puritan immigrants.

Love has played a still smaller part. Smooth courtship has always paid dividends, and it has not always been simply a case of marriage by capture. Only a few primitive societies that have survived down to modern times have been so basic. Some Australasian tribesmen have used barbless arrows to shoot through the legs of the maiden of their choice; they remove them when they have taken the girl home. Another method of direct courtship used in the same area was for the man, if turned down on first approaching his intended mate, to wait for her to lie down to sleep and then crawl forward and poke her breasts with a sharply pointed stick. The girl normally failed to see the compliment behind the action, cursed, moved and tried to get back to sleep again. The determined suitor would follow, stick at the ready and start again. Although it might take a month or two of steady courtship, the wretched, bruised and sleepless girl usually gave in and became the wife of the suitor. It must have been one of the few occasions when a girl spent her wedding day looking forward to the bliss of a comparatively undisturbed night!

Marriage by capture has always excited the minds of male historians and cartoonists. The mild husband dominated by the shrewish wife dreams of himself as a cave man, masterfully knocking the young beauty next door over the head and dragging her off to make her his mate. However, marriage by capture was at least legal in England until the thirteenth century, and it has been suggested that the traditional song "Here We Go Gathering Nuts in May" is a reference to the practice. But it is unlikely that this was ever the normal way of establishing a marriage except where unusual circumstances such as war or natural disaster had deprived a tribe of its normal source of mates. In matrilocal societies, the husband went to live with his wife's family: not a popular move if you have first stolen the bride. Even in patrilocal societies, where the newly married couple moved into the groom's family, genuine marriage by capture has been rare.

What has developed in a variety of societies is marriage by simulated capture. Here the groom, or his family, select a likely bride and he demonstrates his manhood and readiness to support her and a family by performing some obvious feat of manliness or worldliness. Thus he, and his supporters, might seize the chosen girl against the partly simulated resistance of her family and their supporters.

The necessity to seize a bride forcibly stems partly from the value of the girl to her family, emotionally and economically, but it also has a sexual basis. In many societies chastity is a valuable commodity and a girl is taught from her earliest days to resist losing her virginity. This carries on in some cases even after she has married. Among the Koryak, a Siberian tribe living around Kamchatka, the groom has to seize the bride when her father is satisfied with the period of free service the groom has performed for him. The bride's mother warns her that from now on she is liable to be taken. Accordingly the girl summons her friends to help her tie up her sleeves and trousers firmly with thongs in such a way that they can only be cut off her. When approached by her bridegroom she will make every effort to avoid him, fighting him off vigorously if he closes with her. He for his part will pursue and grapple with her until he has been able to cut the thongs, tear off her clothes and touch her sexual organs with his hand. She will immediately become his submissive and willing partner and lead him to her tent. This whole performance is in fact their wedding ceremony.

When capture is the expected, indeed the only respectable, mode of getting married it tends to become less real and more stylized or ceremonial as time goes on. In the old North Western provinces of India the young Kanjar groom would call together his father and male friends and arm them with old muskets, swords, sticks, stones, pots and pans. Making as much threatening noise as possible they would descend upon the house of the chosen bride and surround it, demanding that her family surrender her, upon pain of attacking and beatings. The bride's family would at first answer just as boldly, but eventually allowed the domineering groom's party to overcome them and then handed over the bride, bitterly lamenting. In other parts of India, the party carrying off the bride might be followed by all the women of the district pelting them with mud and abusing them with a picturesque use of foul language.

With all these dramatic and prolonged wedding ceremonies one can only feel that day-to-day life must have seemed rather flat ever after; except, of course, that there were friends' weddings to look forward to.

Most tribal societies that have been studied over the last two centuries, or of which there exists some decipherable record, have been extremely complex in their social organization, and nowhere more so than in the case of who could marry whom. The English consider themselves a class-ridden society but they are nothing compared to some societies where a man or woman may belong to six or seven different classification groups according to their family, their religion, their work, their totem and so on. Each of these areas will have attached to it traditional rules that lay down who a member of that group may or may not marry. For example, it may be that a girl cannot marry any direct relative up to third cousin, nor anyone connected with the families of those people, even adopted children or servants. She will probably have to marry within her religious group, but may not be permitted to marry within her own tribe or members of the same totem. In the end the rules are so strict and far-reaching, and groups so intermingled, that there exists only a limited number of people whom she is ever likely to meet that she may marry. The same, of course, is true of the men in her society.

Traditional hunting lands, agricultural land, houses, animals and the services and religious loyalty of the children pass in most societies from father to son. In quite a number, however, they pass from mother to daughter. In patrilinear societies, the bride generally goes to the groom's tribe and family. The rights over the woman that are transferred to the groom, or to his family, are usually rights to services: economic, domestic, ritual and sexual. The woman is allotted a plot of land to grow the products which are her responsibility and at times she is expected to help with the farm work. Her main duties are concerned with the care of her husband, children and home, the provision of fuel and water, the preparation of food and the washing of clothes. The important religious or ritual posts are all held by men, except insofar as they take place in or around the home, where the women come into their own and direct operations.

In such societies, the bride has before her marriage carried out many of her duties in her father's household and has contributed to the economic success of his family unit. In losing a daughter he loses an economic asset and the groom's family gains one. As is the normal way of the world, those gaining the asset are expected to pay for it, hence marriage by purchase; the payment is known as bridewealth or bride

The Babylonian Marriage Market, *by Edwin Long, an extreme (and once upon a time titillating) view of the mercenary aspects of marriage.*

price. Indeed, the very word *wed* is linked with such words as gage and wage; the wedding is based, etymologically at least, more firmly in economics than most couples may realize. The bride price can be given in the form of various services performed by the groom for the bride's male relatives as is the case with the Taita of Kenya. Or it can be paid in the form of livestock, rats, chickens, goats and cattle, as practiced by the Gisu who live on the slopes of Mount Elgon in East Africa. There is a well-established rate of exchange—six goats equal one cow and the economic system is open to exploitation by the bright young entrepreneur. This is made clear by the Gisu father who tells his young son, "go out and trap rats, exchange them for a cock and a hen, and when you have tended them and have enough chickens exchange them for a nanny and a billy goat. When you have enough goats exchange them for a cow in calf. When you have enough cows to pay the bride price, marry, have a son and set him to trapping rats."

The concept of the bride price is, of course, by no means confined to Africa. In Arab countries the burden of the bride price has been heavy, sometimes equalling one third of the father's annual income. Among the Dayaks of Borneo, as among some Buddhist communities, there is no formal marriage ceremony. The marriage is deemed to have taken place when the bride price has been paid.

The opposite system, the payment of a groom price is perhaps more widespread still. The dowry system was common throughout Europe, particularly for the wealthy and landed classes. It is still practiced in parts of Italy, Greece and France. Here it is assumed that the groom is conferring an honor upon the bride's family by marrying her, and he is rewarded. In India, among the Hindus, there were other factors that helped create the custom of paying a groom price. Early Hindu religious teachers had laid great stress on the necessity for marrying young girls off very early, and considerable penalties were laid down for those who failed in this duty. Unmarried, the girl did not undergo the ritual purification and was on a par with the lowest class. It was thought that if she did not marry before puberty, then her father, mother or eldest brother would go to hell. Faced by this painful and gloomy prospect, the parents of a young girl were only too eager to purchase a bridegroom. It was also possible for a girl to raise her status by marrying into a sub-caste slightly higher than her own. Naturally her parents were expected to pay for the privilege. This system was sometimes abused, particularly by the Bengali Kulin Brahmins, a priestly caste, in the early part of the nineteenth century. Some Kulins were prepared to marry up to twenty wives, at a price, and one is reported to have achieved eighty. In the interests of peace and quiet he did not have his wives living at his home but kept up an annual progress visiting each of them in turn at her father's house and receiving a substantial gift each time for his ineffable condescension. The situation in India today is different of course but in the 1960s a well-educated groom could still command a dowry of between 5 and 50 thousand rupees in some circles.

As girls and boys are fairly evenly distributed in large families, the dowries brought in by the sons roughly balanced the dowries paid out through daughters but girls of poor families, particularly those with no brothers, faced a dismal future. In Athens in 350 B.C., Apollodorus, acting as advocate in a case against a courtesan, called upon the court to "take thought also for women of citizen birth, to see that the daughters of the poor do not become old maids. For as things are now, even if a girl be quite without means, the law sees to the provision of a sufficient dowry for her, if nature has endowed her with an appearance even passably moderate; but if you acquit this woman, drag the law through the mud and render it ineffective, then, without doubt, poverty will force the citizens' daughters to become prostitutes, those for whom a marriage cannot be procured." In Greek society of that time nobody would fail to give a girl a dowry if at all possible. Relatives would provide for nieces, collections were made among the friends of the poor and now and again the state would reward a man for outstanding public service by giving dowries to his daughters.)

The idea of capturing a wife or of obtaining one by paying some kind of price for her does not at first sight tie in with our present-day view of woman occupying an equal place in society with man. It carries with it the concept of woman as an object, a second-class citizen. In some societies this may have been, or be, the case, but in many the status of women was enhanced by the paying of a worthwhile bride price and the woman felt pride and an increased status because her husband had paid over to her relatives objects that had considerable value in the eyes of their society. It gave her the public assurance that she was a person of worth. Marriage by capture, if it were truly just the seizing and ravishing of an object sexually desired, would undoubtedly lower the status of women but we have seen that this was very rarely the case. It was in fact an elaborate ceremony marking the passing of the man and woman from their position as junior members of two family groups to their new position as a comprehensive family unit of their own creation. What is captured or stolen away is almost always an object of value regarded with envy or desire by those who do not possess it. A woman who is "captured" either by force or cunning is therefore publicly recognized as being an object of value, a person of status in her society. Neither purchase nor capture may appeal to the modern woman, but they do not necessarily imply that the women in the societies where they have been current have been demeaned by them.

The status of women has perhaps been most disregarded, not to say abused, in those societies who have either indulged in child marriages, or binding betrothals, or who have used marriages as a form of creating alliances between families for the purpose of increasing wealth and power. By and large this form of behavior has not been practiced in so-called primitive societies but has developed in civilized societies. We have certainly not seen the end of it today, and both women and men can be pawns in weddings whose basis may be economic, dynastic or political.

The wedding ceremony, wherever it takes place in the world, is almost always a ritual act. Within it there are still elements of magic, morals and the law. Each of these is symbolically represented in various parts of the ritual or ceremony.

Marriage is primarily a survival mechanism for mankind in that it allows for the continuity of the race against a secure background and within social regulations. It is therefore widely hoped that the wedding will result in a fruitful union. The production of the "fruit" still requires sexual activity. Sex is surrounded by taboos. Part of the wedding ritual is concerned either with modifying these taboos or with replacing pre-wedding taboos with new post-wedding taboos.

Fertility is most obviously symbolized by the fruits of the earth. In many wedding rituals fruit, grain and cereals are thrown over the bride and groom or over their bed. Another obvious symbol is a child itself and many wedding ceremonies call for the bride to be accompanied by a small child.

Physical fears of a painful defloration or a troublesome childbirth lead to rituals designed to improve these situations. The breaking of some object forms a part of many wedding rites and this is intended to ease the breaking of the hymen through sympathetic magic. In a similar way, rituals involving the loosening of knots and laces, which also occur in a lot of ceremonies, are intended to ease the pangs of childbirth.

Primitive man relied upon the earth and the sky for survival; they were the two most powerful forces within his comprehension. Sometimes they rewarded him, sometimes they punished him. The resemblance between his relationship with them and his own with his small children was obvious. In man's early magic, therefore, the Earth Mother and the Sky Father assumed all-important roles. Mother had seeds implanted within her and was then fertilized with rain from Father. In a number of early languages the words for plough and penis, seed and semen, furrow and vagina, the generation of seeds and of children were the same.

As has always happened, man tried to have some influence on events outside his direct control by using sympathetic magic. He created rituals whereby a man represented Sky and a woman represented Earth. The aim of the ritual was to produce bountiful crops so the man and the woman standing in for the God and Goddess had to copulate, either actually or symbolically. This, it was believed, created power which would be beneficial to the weather and to the crops. Naturally the authority and power vested in the couple who performed this ritual was considerable. In time it grew and extended beyond the period immediately surrounding the ceremony itself and the couple began to be recognized first as the spiritual rulers of the community and, eventually, as its temporal rulers, its King and Queen. The ritual of sacred copulation became a royal wedding ceremony carried out with high religious overtones.

Many accounts of such ceremonies exist throughout history and the echoes continue up until today: in the Brahmin wedding ceremony the bridegroom says to the bride, "I am the sky, thou art the earth; come, let us marry," a very direct reference back to the early days of myth and magic.

The concept of the union of sun/sky and earth is found in most areas of the world. In Transylvania neolithic figurines have been found, believed to be of magic significance, representing copulating couples. One arm of one of the pair points to the sky, one arm of the other points to the earth. In Bengal, the Oraons celebrated the wedding of the sun and the earth every year. They bathed and then carried their priest to his house, which had been decorated lavishly with greenery and flowers. There he underwent the form of marriage with his wife which represented the union of sun and earth. After the wedding the people feasted and made love to each other freely in the hope of setting the crops a good example of fruitfulness. The American Indians have similar beliefs. The Pueblo Indians act out a symbolic marriage between earth and sky wherein a man is appointed as the "Silent One" and has symbolic intercourse with a virgin in order to secure the blessings of the earth. During the Arapaho sun dance there comes a moment when the woman who symbolically represents the "mother of the tribe" has intercourse with a priest representing God in order to promote the growth of the tribe. In the Arapaho's offerings lodge there were two pieces of turf which represented father and mother, sky and earth.

In Africa the Masai refer to the sky lying on the earth like a man making love to his wife, and the divine King of the Bemba, in northern Rhodesia, used to have intercourse with his chief wife only when carrying out the fertility ritual which was designed to increase the fruitfulness of the tribe's crops and women. In Morocco, among some Berber tribes, there is a spring ceremony in which a girl and a young man are chosen to be the "Bride and Bridegroom of the Good." After being dressed as for a wedding they are shut together in the mosque where the young man sacrifices a cock and then has intercourse with his "Bride." Later the young couple are symbolically killed and restored to life. This ceremony is believed to bring about a good year for the village concerned.

All over the world, therefore, we can find evidence of forms of magical or sacred wedding ceremonies that were seen to be essential to the survival of the community. In many cases a couple was chosen to represent the supernatural forces and they became rulers of the community in their own right. The wedding ceremony also conferred upon them the status of monarch. The wedding ceremony was a *de facto* coronation ceremony. Some authorities see the Christian wedding ceremony as being royal in origin and as reenacting in part the old ceremony of coronation. Certainly the coronation of a queen used to take place at her wedding. When King Ethelwulf married Judith in 856, his French bride was crowned during the ceremony, as was Queen Hermintrude at Soissons ten years later.

When first the nobility and later the merchants came to celebrate their weddings with ritual, apeing their rulers, they adopted the appearance of royalty. Over the years the commoners began to mark their own unions with similar ceremonies. They wore ceremonial clothing or decorations, were often crowned, as they still are in Burma, Greece, Russia and parts of Eastern Europe, and were generally treated as royalty for the period of the wedding ceremony. These royal customs generally, if not always, existed before either Christianity or Islam began to influence social behavior, and in many instances have been adopted into the developing religious wedding ceremony.

The following chapters show how old pagan rites were practiced, and how in modified form they have survived. From ancient times the wedding ceremony has grown, absorbing constantly from different cultures, into that most usually observed in Britain and the United States today, and as we follow its progress we may see also how the occasion of marriage is celebrated in other countries: how primitive custom and superstition are evident not only in the practices of still primitive and superstitious peoples, but also, however vestigially, in our own.

"Buying a new wife in the Stone Age," by W. Heath Robinson.

WHEN IN ROME...AND IN ATHENS

*"Fair concord, ever abide by their couch, and to so well-matched
a pair may Venus ever be propitious"* MARTIAL

WE HAVE INHERITED so much from the great civilizations of
Rome and Greece that it is no surprise to discover echoes of their
wedding ceremonies in our own. The Roman bride, for example, wore a
veil, was presented with a wedding ring, ate a special cake as part of the
religious ceremony, had rice thrown over her and was carried over the
threshold of her new home by her bridegroom.

The arrival of the newly married couple at their house was a very
significant moment, for to the Romans the home was a temple, and in it
dwelt the *lares*, the family's divine spirits, as well as its living members.
For a man to bring a bride to his home—someone, that is, who was no
part of the family—meant that she had to be accepted by those spirits.
Until that acceptance was assured, the wedding could not be said to have
taken place. She had to enter the family, therefore, in such a way as to be
able to share in its *sacra*, that is the worship of the household spirits, of
the ancestors in their tombs or in any special cult attached to the family.
In order to ensure that this was done and the approval of the gods secured,
a sacrificial ceremony was carried out, called *confarreatio*, whereby the
bride was transferred from the absolute control of her father to that of
her husband as the head of the new family.

At this ceremony a sacred cake, made of an Italian grain called
far, was eaten by the bride and groom. The cake was dedicated to Jupiter
Farreus and it is probable that the god was believed to live in the cake so
that he was absorbed by both bride and groom, thus consecrating their
union. This ceremony, which took place in the presence of the Pontifex
Maximus, the Flamen Dialis (priest of Jupiter) and ten witnesses, was
only undertaken by patricians. Plebeian marriages were marked by the
ceremony of *coemptio*, a kind of fictitious sale made in the presence of not
less than five witnesses who had to be Roman citizens over the age of
puberty. By this ceremony, the bride's father "mancipated" his
daughter to her husband. A third ceremony, known as *usus*, could legally

join a plebeian man to a patrician woman; all that was required of them was that they should cohabit uninterruptedly for a year.

All these forms of wedding ceremony had died out of Roman society by the second century A.D., but the family was still very important and much legislation was drafted to cover all aspects of married life. The main body of Roman law was codified by the order of the emperor Justinian and in one of its principal parts, the "Digest," it defines marriage to be "the union of a man and woman forming an association during their entire lives, and involving the common enjoyment of divine and human privileges."

The "Digest" also has something to say on betrothals, which had become fashionable.

In contracting a betrothal, there is no limit to the age of the parties, as is the case in marriage. Wherefore, a betrothal can be made at a very early age, provided what is being done is understood by both persons, that is to say, where they are not under seven years of age. A betrothal, like a marriage, is made with the consent of the contracting parties, and therefore, as is the case of marriage, a son under parental control must agree to it. A girl who evidently does not resist the will of her father is understood to give her consent. A daughter is permitted to refuse to consent to her father's wishes only when he selects someone for her husband who is unworthy on account of his habits or who is of infamous character.

Betrothals, as such, carried no real obligations. The boy and girl, with the consent of their fathers, would state their intention publicly before a gathering of friends and relatives, some of whom would act as witnesses. The young man would present the girl with gifts and a ring of iron or gold, which she would immediately place on her ring finger. After that there would be a feast and merrymaking. Betrothals and marriages were rarely the result of romantic love. They were seen to be vehicles for service to the family and to the state.

On the day of her wedding a Roman bride would lay aside the *toga praetexta* of her childhood and would dedicate her dolls to the *lar* of the family. She would then put on a tunic without a hem and tie a woolen girdle around her waist, fastening it with a special double knot called the knot of Hercules. Over her tunic she wore a cloak of saffron yellow and on her feet sandals of the same color. Around her neck she would clasp a metal necklace. Her hair was dressed and six pads of

In this marriage scene the bride and groom clasp hands over a sacred flame, with Juno in the background as the bride's pronuba. *From a Roman sarcophagus, third century A.D.*

artificial hair were added, separated by narrow bands such as the Vestal Virgins wore. Over this elaborate piece of styling she wore a veil of red or yellow material which half-covered her face. On the crown of her head she wore a wreath of myrtle and orange blossom.

Dressed thus she stood with her family and welcomed the wedding guests and her groom. When everybody was assembled, a sacrifice would be made, usually a sheep or a pig, and the entrails would be examined to see if the auspices were favorable. If they were, the young couple would be directed to join their right hands by the *pronuba*, a respectable married woman who acted as a kind of priestess for the occasion. Hands joined, the bride and groom would publicly pledge themselves to each other. The wedding was now over and the assembled guests would all crowd around and congratulate the happy pair while those who had acted as witnesses would affix their personal seals to the marriage contract.

Everyone would then be summoned to the wedding feast, which would last until nightfall, when it was time to escort the bride to her new home. The procession was headed by flute players and five torch bearers. The bride was led by each hand by a young boy whose parents must be living, while a third went immediately in front of her carrying the nuptial torch, made up from tightly twisted hawthorn twigs. As the procession, singing lustily, and sometimes lewdly, neared the groom's house, nuts were thrown to the children as a symbol of future fertility. As the Roman house was a temple as well as a home, the doorway marked the dividing line between the sacred and the profane and special observances had to be made before the bride crossed the threshold, over which was spread a white cloth strewn with leaves and branches. On arriving, the bride smeared the doorposts with fat and oil and tied a strand of wool around each. She was then lifted over the threshold by her new husband, followed immediately by three bridesmaids. One carried her distaff and one her spindle, obvious symbols of her virtue and dedication to domestic duties. The third waited until the groom had offered the bride fire and water, the essentials of domestic life, and then led her to the bridal couch where the groom would invite the bride to lie down. He would then remove her cloak and begin the task of untying the double knot of Hercules while the guests withdrew.

Eros visiting a bride: fragment of a terracotta relief from Tarentum, fifth century B.C.

Aristotle, writing about the past, illustrated the growing sophistication of Greek society by looking at marriage patterns. "That improvement has occurred is shown by the fact that the old customs were exceedingly simple and barbarous. For the ancient Hellenes went about armed and bought their brides off each other." Demosthenes, who died in the same year as Aristotle, gave the up-to-date picture. "For this is matrimony, when a man begets children, and introduces the sons to members of his clan and township, and affiances his daughters to their husbands as his own. . . . Mistresses we keep for pleasure, concubines for daily attendance upon our person, wives to bear us legitimate children and be our faithful housekeepers." Like the Romans, the Greeks took a wife to ensure the continuance of their family and the ongoing worship of their family gods. If the marriage could also strengthen their wealth and social position, so much the better. Romance did not enter into it.

A variety of laws covered the arrangement and celebration of a marriage. It was laid down that there should be a betrothal when the girl's father or guardian pledged her to her future husband. This was a formal act carried out in front of witnesses from both families. At the same ceremony it was decided what the bride's dowry was to be. The bride and groom were very likely to be related, for families liked to keep property within the clan. It was common for uncles to marry their nieces and half-brothers their half-sisters. To ignore a suitable cousin as a prospective marriage partner would have been considered insulting.

Men married at about thirty, the age at which they would assume the duties of head of the family from their fathers. Girls married much younger, largely because of the fanatical importance the Greeks gave to virginity; the average age was between sixteen and eighteen. Until recent times more girl babies than boy babies have survived infancy and frequent wars meant that many young men were cut off in their prime. There were always more girls than men, therefore, and the competition for husbands was intense as it was a man's duty to marry off his daughters and his sisters. The dowry that a girl could bring with her was consequently very important, and it was a matter of honor for a family to provide as large a dowry as possible. It usually consisted of cash or of land and property valued in cash and, apart from its value as a sign of social status, was intended primarily for a woman's maintenance. The dowry remained in the husband's control while he lived but if he died first it was returned with the widow to her own family and would act as the dowry for her second marriage, for widows were remarried as soon as possible. If there had been children by the marriage, then the dowry was theirs, or went to their male guardians if they were under age, always provided they supported their mother.

When the dowry had been settled a marriage contract could be signed. The existence of such a contract owed much to Roman and Egyptian influence and showed that women's status in Greece during Aristotle's time was slowly improving. The following is a translation of a marriage contract from the year 311 B.C.

Heracleides takes Demetria of Cos as his lawful wife. He received her from her father, Leptine of Cos, and from her mother, Philotis.

He is a free man and she a free woman. She brings with her clothes and jewels worth 1,000 drachmas. Heracleides will provide Demetria with all the requirements of a free woman. They shall live in whatever place seems best to Leptine and Heracleides.

If Demetria is found to have done something which disgraces her husband she shall lose everything she brought with her. And Heracleides shall accuse her before three men chosen by both of them. Heracleides shall not be permitted to wrong Demetria by keeping another woman or having children by another woman, nor to harm Demetria in any way under any pretext. If Heracleides is found to have done such a thing, Demetria shall accuse him before three men whom they both have chosen. Heracleides shall then repay to Demetria the 1,000 drachmas, in Alexandrian silver, as recompense.

This contract, in that it places restrictions on the husband, is in advance of contracts written at that time in mainland Greece. Heracleides and Demetria lived in the Greek society of Egypt and she benefited from the higher status that women had there.

When the dowry had been agreed and the contract signed, arrangements for the wedding could be made, although it was likely to be postponed until a propitious month. The month in which the anniversary of Zeus' marriage to Hera was celebrated was the most popular. The wedding ceremony lasted for three days. On the first day the bride made a sacrifice to Zeus and Hera and to the Fates. It was important that, during this sacrifice, no bile be spilled on the altar or the marriage would be marred by excessive quarreling. The bridegroom made a similar sacrifice and then a procession would be formed to lead the young couple to the bath house. The procession was led by flute players and torch bearers, and they carried the bath water with them. A young male child would carry a special jar for the bathing of the groom and then of the bride by their attendants.

On the second day the bride's house was decorated with greenery and flowers and she was dressed by her friends and attendants. She wore a loose robe and simply knotted girdle and on her head she wore a veil topped with a crownlike wreath of myrtle.

On her feet she wore special bridal sandals. After the wedding ceremony, the guests were invited to a feast at which the most important item was a pie made of sesame seeds, which symbolized the future fruitfulness of the newly married couple. At the end of the wedding feast, the bride ceremoniously removed her veil and revealed her face. The groom would respond by presenting her with special "revelation" gifts.

The young couple would now be led in procession to the bridegroom's house. The procession would be headed by a man bearing a staff, the bride and groom would follow, then the family carrying torches, and finally the other guests and children wearing wreaths and playing flutes. The groom would lift the bride into his chariot and they would be driven away. On arriving at his house, the groom would grasp the bride by her wrist and lead her to the doorway where his parents would be waiting to greet her, father standing on the threshold and mother close by, holding a torch. As the bride crossed the threshold, the guests threw nuts and fruit over them in yet another fertility rite. Once inside, the bride was presented with a sieve, a coffee-roaster and a pestle as the insignia of her new domestic duties, and was led formally around the hearth. She was then led to the bridal chamber which was guarded by one of the groom's companions. Gathered outside the doorway, as the groom loosened the bridal garments, the children sang *epithalamia*, wedding songs such as Sappho wrote:

Maidenhood, O Maidenhood　　　　*Bridegroom dear, to what shall I*
Where art thou flown away from me?　*compare thee?*
Never again shall I come back,　　　*To a slim green rod best do I*
Never again back to thee.　　　　　*compare thee.*

The next day children carrying torches would call at the bridegroom's house, bringing gifts; usually these were a cloak for the groom and jewelry for the bride. In the week that followed, it was customary for the bridegroom to visit his father-in-law's house and spend the night there lying beside a little girl whose parents had to be alive. The bride remained at the groom's house and lay beside a little boy. This custom was supposed to show that although the bride had been separated from her family by the wedding ceremony the married couple were now formally reunited with her family as a pair.

The circumstances surrounding the celebration of marriage in Greece today, and in the fairly recent past, do not vary all that much in essence from the ceremonies of classical Greece. The Christian element has been introduced but, as in many societies, the strictly religious part of the wedding ceremony does not have the importance, in the eyes of the ordinary person, that the traditional rites have. It must be remembered also that Greece has been subjected to a long period of Turkish domination, is geographically divided into a large number of necessarily separate communities and is populated by a people who have had to struggle hard to survive. The sense of community is strong and customs are preserved fiercely as a form of local identity. Wedding customs throughout Greece vary considerably, therefore, although they have a common base. It is impossible to describe them all in detail but an impressionistic picture can be put together by describing some of the more colorful from a variety of social and geographical backgrounds.

An observer of Greek high society in the early 1900s was a guest at the wedding of the son of an ex-prime minister to the daughter of a well-known statesman. As was then the fashion it took place at the house of the bride at 9.30 in the evening. The ballroom had been turned into a chapel and the Metropolitan of Athens conducted the service assisted by three priests. The service embraced two ceremonies, that of both betrothal and marriage, which used to be carried out separately.

The ceremony began with two five-foot-high candles being lighted. These were adorned with white satin ribbons and sprigs of orange blossom and were held by the bride's brother and a lady. The bride and groom stood in front of the table being used as an altar, on which lay a copy of the Gospels. The Metropolitan took up two rings and made the sign of the cross upon the Bible, and he then touched the brows of the young couple with them three times, saying "the servant of God is betrothed" on each occasion. Next he put the rings on their hands. Then the chief bridesmaid, a married lady, changed the rings three times, a ritual normally carried out by the best man.

The betrothal completed, the wedding ceremony began. Psalms and prayers were read, while one of the priests held the triple candle, which is used in church services, on one side of the table and another held the double candle on the other side. The Metropolitan took the two crowns, garlands of artificial flowers, which are always tied together with white ribands, and placed them, thus united, on the heads of the bride and groom. The crowns were changed over by the best man and by the chief bridesmaid. The Metropolitan then took up a cup of wine, which represents the wine drunk at the marriage at Canaan. In church, consecrated wine is used, in a house, unconsecrated. The young couple were given three spoonfuls of wine apiece and the best man also received a spoonful. A prayer was then made that the groom might be magnified like Abraham and the bride like Sarah. The ceremony was then brought to an end by the pair walking three times around the altar, followed by their immediate attendants, as the guests pelted them with rose leaves.

While this was the way of society in 1900, peasant weddings in the country were much more colorful and filled with ritual. There the bridegroom would go by mule to fetch his bride back to his village accompanied by his friends. A bagpiper would lead the returning procession, closely followed by the groom and his companions, then by the bride. It was the custom to pretend that she had been dragged from her mother's side by force and she was not allowed to speak or to move unduly. Escorting her on foot would be the maidens with whom she had played as a young girl, while her father and other male relatives would follow on their mules. Finally would come the mules bearing her all-important dowry: rugs, dresses, quilts, bags, scarves, distaff and spindle—all displayed as advantageously as possible to strike the beholder full of wonder and envy.

After the religious ceremony, the young couple would be pelted with sweets as they walked down the aisle wearing their crowns, each carrying a candle. When they stepped outside the church, the young men of the village would raise their rifles and fire a volley at the sky. They would then walk to the groom's house with their crowns carried before them on a tray. At his house the groom would enter and shut the door. The bride would be lifted from her mule, a perfectly new rug would be spread across it, and she was passed backward and forward across it three or four times. The bride, still silent and with eyes downcast, would then be led to the threshold, where honey was smeared on the middle of the door. She then stepped back a little way and hurled a ripe pomegranate at the patch of honey. The idea was to get some of the seeds to stick to the honey. When this had been done, the bridegroom opened the door and offered the bride bread and salt, which she took and ate outside the door. She would then touch oil and water, after which the bridegroom would carry her over the threshold and place her in a corner with her back to the wall. Here all her dowry would be piled around her like presents at the foot of a Christmas tree.

The feasting would then begin and would probably last until the small hours of the morning. During all this time the bride was not allowed to speak, move or even raise her eyes. She had to remain silent and unmoved until the last guest had left the house, and even then she could not change her position until the bridegroom had given her permission.

The general pattern had not changed very greatly by the 1950s although customs varied. The church ceremony still contained many elements that owed their origins to pagan practice rather than to true

A bride at her toilet. As she combs her hair, her mother is in attendance with her ribbon. Attic red-figure vase, fifth century B.C.

Christianity: the priest joined the couple's hands, a memory of the groom's grasping the wrist of his bride; the crowns were a direct descendent of the ancient wreath; the walking round the altar, known as the dance of Isaiah, recalled the circling of the domestic fire, home of the household gods. And the pelting of the newly married pair with sugared almonds, rice or rose leaves is obviously a symbolic fertility rite and an appeal to the old gods.

In some parts of Greece the procession to the groom's house is showered with rice, cottonseed, small coins and myrtle leaves as well as with sweets. When the procession arrives at the door of the house, the bride dismounts from the cart or mule upon which she has ridden and the axle or the saddle is smashed. This stems from the old Boeotian custom of burning the axle before the door of the groom's house, a piece of sympathetic magic aimed at ensuring that the bride stays where she has been put down. In some areas the groom's parents still greet the bride at the threshold. The mother gives the bride a small pot of honey into which she dips her fingers and then makes the sign of the cross upon the door. The old wedding pie still survives in a slightly changed form on Crete, where the bride is given a pastry made from honey, walnuts and sesame seeds. This, it is hoped, will ensure a sweet, i.e., prosperous and fruitful life. In other rites associated with fertility, probably of both the crops and the couple, the bride jumps over a sieve or a plowshare or scatters wheat or pomegranate seeds across the threshold and inside the house. On the third day of the wedding festivities the bride, in many places, is led in procession to the village spring or well and draws water. On her way home she stops and offers water to those of her fellow villagers whom she meets and they, in turn, drop small coins into her pitcher. Water is of the greatest importance to the Greek villagers and they frequently boast proudly of the coolness and quality of their spring. By drawing the water of life, the bride marks her entrance to her new role and its accompanying domestic duties.

Although the major cities of Greece are as modern as any other in Europe and the life of the city dweller appears to be similar to that of his opposite number in Germany or England, the basic assumptions about the relationship between men and women are still very much as they were a hundred, or a thousand, years ago. This is, of course, more apparent in the small villages but the underlying values are much the same throughout Greece. Parents still have a great deal to say in the choosing of marriage partners and there is little freedom in the relationship of young men and women. A woman's honor is still jealously preserved and a girl who has lost her virginity can expect her brother to react by beating up her seducer or to punish her severely if he thinks she was equally guilty. Even now that young men and women can meet casually they behave with exaggerated propriety and often rely on their parents to make their marriage arrangements even if they suggest the name of the partner themselves. The dowry is still a matter of great importance, and a young girl who has no father or close male relative to provide one can usually resign herself to being an old maid, a fate which the Greeks regard with dismay.

Once the match has been agreed upon, the couple become engaged by exchanging rings in the presence of family and friends, an occasion for the exchange of toasts and feasting. This ceremony is as binding as marriage but allows the young couple no licence. Even if the actual wedding day is a year away they do not use the time to get to know each other better but rather to consolidate their worldly position. The young man works hard and saves what he can. The girl and her female relatives work even harder, adding to their usual tasks that of preparing the dowry.

Weddings usually take place on a Sunday. On the previous Wednesday there is the ritual of "starting the leaven." In both homes, relatives are invited to come and watch freshly milled flour being sieved by a boy and a girl. When enough flour has been sieved, the watchers break their silence and cast coins into the sieve with cries of "good luck." The dough is mixed with pure water and three shots are fired to let the village know that this stage in the preceedings has been reached. Dough is smeared onto the bride or groom's face and dinner is served to the guests in each home. Afterwards the groom's party go happily over to the bride's house and the two parties dance, drink toasts and discharge their rifles into the air.

Thursday is spent quietly, no doubt with a certain nursing of hangovers, but on Friday the dowry is laid out in the bride's house and the village women visit to wonder over it. They bring with them small gifts of basil, cotton and rice. Once the dowry has been admired by everyone, the ceremony known as the "filling of the sacks" commences. The bride's mother puts a copper saucepan in the bottom of a sack and then the bride fills it, and other sacks, with all her worldly goods while the visitors throw coins in among them. Then her bedding is stacked up, with her friends strewing rice and pinning sweet-smelling herbs to it. All duties done, the bride's friends dance in her courtyard. While this is going on, the groom sends a pitcher of wine around the village to his friends and relatives, together with a written invitation to the wedding feast. The bride's father does the same and, on the Saturday morning, the bride goes with some of her friends to ask the young girls of the village to come to her wedding. She gives them sweets instead of wine.

The great day dawns and all the village goes to church as usual, but afterwards the girls go to the bride's home to dance as she dresses for the wedding, while the boys do the same for the groom. An escort is then sent from the groom's home to fetch that most important man at a Greek wedding, the *koumbaros* or sponsor. He is almost always the groom's godfather, though occasionally another man will be nominated as a mark of great honor. When the *koumbaros* arrives, a white flag decorated with sweet herbs and apples is raised over the groom's house. The procession is now ready to start for the bride's house; a young man carrying the flag leads, followed by the priest and the groom's family.

At the bride's home, the flag bearer flies the banner from her roof and is rewarded with a ring biscuit from the bride. On the threshold the groom is offered wine and a buttonhole of herbs by the bride's mother. He kisses her hand and she kisses him on both cheeks. He then drinks the wine and fixes the buttonhole to his lapel. The bride now leaves for the church on the arm of a male relative while the rest of the party follow on foot. After the religious ceremony, with the exchange of rings and crowns, comes the Dance of Isaiah. The priest holds the Bible in one hand and the hand of the groom in the other. The groom grasps the hand of the bride and she does the same to the *koumbaros*. They then circle the table, upon which the wreaths have been laid, three times, stopping four times on each circuit. The wedding guests shower them with rice and sugared almonds with great vigor all this time. Decorum is eventually restored as the wedding party faces the priest in front of the altar while he reads the scripture to them and gives them his blessing.

As the bride reaches the groom's house after the church service, the flag is re-erected above it, and she throws a piece of old iron onto the roof in symbolic representation of strength in her new home. Her new mother-in-law then gives her a ring biscuit. The bride holds it up above her head and breaks it into four pieces. She eats one, puts two on her breast and gives one to her mother-in-law, who offers her a glass of wine in return. She makes the sign of the cross with the wine and returns the glass. A young boy, whose parents are living, is then passed up to her and she sits him on her lap, kisses him, gives him sweets and hangs a ring biscuit around his neck. This hopefully guarantees her male children. That settled, she dismounts from her horse assisted by her brother-in-law or some other close male relative of her husband's who will turn her around three times before setting her upon the ground.

When the dowry has been unpacked and displayed and the guests seated before the groaning tables, the dancing can begin. The father of the groom will give money to the musicians and name a dance which he will lead in honor of the bride. The bride's nearest male relative will give money to the musicians, name his dance and lead it in honor of first the groom and then the bride. After this it is the turn of the *koumbaros* and such other members of the party as wish to honor the young couple.

The Greeks have a great capacity for enjoying themselves and a remarkable degree of stamina. To attend a Greek wedding in the country is a memorable if somewhat exhausting experience. It can also be quite an awe-inspiring one if you consider how many of the customs date back into the days of classical Greece some 2,500 years ago. The basic human requirement for ritual and sympathetic magic associated with this great moment of their lives is obviously very real and amazingly persistent.

The crowning moment in a modern Greek Orthodox wedding.

ABOVE *A nuptial scene from a Roman house fresco, first century B.C.*

RIGHT *Eros, clutching wedding vases, leads the bride and groom in this detail from a Greek wedding vase, fifth century B.C.*

OPPOSITE *Jan van Eyck's* Arnolfini Marriage, *from the National Gallery, London. The artist's declaration, "Johannes de dyck fuit hic," has been taken to suggest that the painting depicts an actual wedding ceremony, and that van Eyck was himself a witness. Early fifteenth century.*

PRECEDING PAGES *Pieter Bruegel may have satirized the life of peasants in the sixteenth-century Netherlands, but he always showed a genuine interest in their customs. Music, drinking and feasting, then as now, made for a successful wedding party.*
RIGHT *William Hogarth, another satirist, shows how fashionable marriages in the eighteenth century were contracted to ensure the continuation of family and fortune. The parents are obviously more concerned with ancestry and finance than the betrothed are with each other. From* Marriage à la Mode, *National Gallery, London.*

ABOVE The Unequal Marriage, *by Vasili Pukirev. "What can a young lassie," asked Robert Burns, "do wi' an auld man?" Marry him for his money, presumably.*

LEFT *Two contrasting French paintings: Greuze's* L'accordée de Village *depicts a humbler marriage contract (Louvre, eighteenth-century); a century earlier Lausmosnier captured all the pomp of court life at the marriage of Louis XIV.*

CAKES AND VEILS

"I sing of May-poles, Hock-carts, Wassails, Wakes,
Of Bride-grooms, Brides and of their Bridal-Cakes" ROBERT HERRICK

PROMETHEUS IS ATTRIBUTED with being the first maker of a ring, the metal being smelted in the fire he stole from Zeus. Adam advised Cain to use one when marrying his wife. This ring was not of gold but of iron adorned with adamant, according to Swinburne's *Treatise of Spouses* (1686), which states that the iron was

> hard and durable, signifying the continuance and perpetuity of the contract; the virtuous adamant, drawing the iron into it, signifying the perfect unity and indissoluble conjunction of their minds, in true and perfect love. Howbeit it skilleth not at this day what metal the ring be: the form of the ring being circular, that is, round, and without end, importeth thus much, that their mutual love and hearty affection should roundly flow from one to another, as in a circle and that continually and for ever.

Certainly, the Romans used iron rings, and the custom was adopted by the Greeks, when they became betrothed. It served a dual purpose; it was a down payment and a sign that a contract had been made and that the woman concerned was no longer for sale. No doubt the Romans brought the custom to Britain where it was certainly well enough established by the fourteenth century for Chaucer to write of the marriage of Griselda in the "Clerk's Tale" of the *Canterbury Tales*:

> *She stood transmuted by her wondrous dress*
> *Almost unrecognized through loveliness,*
> *The Marquis then espoused her with a ring*
> *Bought for the purpose. . . .*

Being given by a marquis, Griselda's ring was probably gold but it need not have been. The early records tell of wedding rings made of iron, steel, silver, copper, brass, leather and rush. The easy availability of rushes, the belief by simple maidens in the legally binding nature of a ring placed on the "wedding" finger and the cunning of lusty young men combined to bring forth an official warning from the Church in the person of Richard Poore, bishop of Salisbury, who published a constitution in 1217 forbidding such wicked young men from having their way with trusting virgins by plaiting a ring of rush and saying "why not, we're married." "Let no man," thundered the bishop, "put a ring of rush, or of any other material, upon the hands of young girls, by way of mock celebration, for the purpose of easily seducing them, that, while believing he is only perpetrating a jest, he may not in reality find himself bound irrevocably to the connubial yoke." If the young man had placed the ring on the girl's finger in the presence of witnesses and had publicly declared that he was taking her for his wife, then the law and the church could regard the marriage as binding—and serve him right, no doubt.

Generally rush rings were for the poor or for the romantic. Considerations of position, and investment, normally ensured that the ring was made of precious metal, although silver was for a long time in more common use than gold. They varied considerably in their design and were often garnished with precious and semi-precious stones. Additional symbolism was called forth in designs that included clasped hands, twin hearts pierced by Cupid's arrow and a single heart held in a loving hand. The likenesses of saints were used to add to the blessings brought by the ring, including that of St. Margaret, the patroness of childbirth. Words, too, were brought into play, once again first by the Romans and Greeks. The poetry used, called poesy, was changed by common speech into "posy," and was engraved upon the inner surface of the ring. Shakespeare mentions this custom in *The Merchant of Venice*:

About a hoop of gold, a paltry ring
That she did give me, whose poesy was
For all the world like cutlers' poetry,
Upon a knife, Love me and leave me not.

Bishop Bull of St. David's had engraved upon his wife's wedding ring the Latin words *Bene parere, parere, parare det mihi Deus*; these certainly look well and have an air of academic jocularity but, on translation, are unlikely to be totally pleasing to the modern wife—"God make me prolific, obedient and sedulous." They are less commonplace, however, than many of the most popular ones used over the centuries such as: "Our contract was heaven's act"; "In thee my choice, I do rejoice"; "I will be yours while breath endures"; "Despise not me, that joys in thee"; and "If you deny, then sure I die." No doubt Samuel Pepys came up with a more distinguished verse on the occasion he noted in his diary: " . . . we sat studying a posy for a ring for her which she is to have at Roger Pepys his wedding."

Another aspect of the wedding ring given much attention by our ancestors was its fit, which had to be perfect. The exactness of the fit on the finger for which the ring had been fashioned represented the nicety and perfect harmony with which a married couple should fit one another in temper, taste and mental capacity.

With the coming to power of the Puritans, the wedding ring, as with most wedding ritual, went out of official favor. Marriage was a serious legal contract between man and woman and should take place before a justice of the peace. Public opinion and quiet determination brought the wedding back into the church before long but the Puritans did not allow the use of the service in the Book of Common Prayer. Instead they instituted a much simplified ceremony laid down in the new *Directory of Public Worship* of 1664. The wedding ring was too obviously a piece of jewelry and therefore an object of Satan. Indeed one Puritan minister referred to it unequivocally as being "a Relique of Popery and a Diabolical Circle for the Devil to Dance in." However, to many people the wedding ring continued to be a necessary part of the wedding ceremony mainly because it was a visible demonstration of the husband's promise to the wife. Some Puritan ministers were brave enough to express their views not only in sermons but in print. In 1658, William Secker published a sermon which was as popular in the American colonies as it was in England. This was entitled "A Wedding Ring Fit for the Finger; or the Salve of Divinity upon the Sore of Humanity; Laid Open in a Sermon at a Wedding in Edmonton." Apart from his stressing the symbolism of the wedding ring, Mr. Secker also conjured up an image from the barnyard. Man and wife, he said, should go through life vying with each other in industry for the good of their children, "even as the cock and hen both scrape in the dust heap to pick

44

up something for their chickens." With the return of the monarchy, and its attendant priests and prelates, to England in 1660 marriage ceremonies generally returned to church and the wedding ring came once more out of hiding—although in America, with its stronger Puritan population, marriage before a magistrate only continued to enjoy legal, ecclesiastical and social approval.

One particular type of ring, the gimmal or double ring, was very popular in the sixteenth and seventeenth centuries throughout Europe and enjoyed particular favor in Germany and Scandinavia. The gimmal ring consisted of two or more hoops that could be worn singly or which could be joined by a clasp or hinge to form one apparently solid ring.

At the time of engagement or betrothal, the gimmal ring would be divided and would be worn by the man and woman. Sometimes, if there were more than two hoops to the gimmal ring, separate hoops would also be given to the witnesses and would be worn by them. At the wedding ceremony, the gimmal ring would be joined together and used as a wedding ring. Dryden referred to this in "Don Sebastian":

> *A curious artist wrought 'em,*
> *With joynts so close as not to be perceiv'd,*
> *Yet are they both each other's counterpart.*
> *(Her part had Juan inscribed, and his had Zayda.*
> *You know the names were theirs:) and in the midst,*
> *A heart divided in two halves was plac'd.*
> *Now if the rivets of those rings, inclosed,*
> *Fit not each other, I have forged this lye:*
> *But if they join, you must for ever part.*

The double ring has enjoyed a tremendous resurgence of popularity over the past three decades in the United States, where today as many as ninety percent of grooms emulate their brides in wearing a wedding ring. Whether a result of contemporary ideas about equality and "togetherness" or merely a result of relaxed opinions about male jewelry, the practice illustrates that the modern ceremony need not sacrifice tradition to rigidity and conformity, that the old customs still survive and flourish or, as in this case, may be revitalized.

The finger upon which the wedding ring is placed is the subject of as much of the myth of symbolism as is any other aspect of the wedding ceremony. Most of it is based upon the belief that the wedding ring has always been worn upon the fourth finger of the left hand, that is the fourth digit, the thumb being the first. This is not the case. During the fifteenth century in certain ecclesiastical provinces in Europe, such as the archbishopric of Bologna, the wedding ring was placed upon the fourth finger of the bride's right hand. That this may have been so in England in the Middle Ages is shown by a reference in Peter Heylyn's *History of the Reformation*, first published in 1661. Here he implies that the custom changed with the Reformation and says that from then on it was the rule "that the man should put the wedding ring on the fourth finger of the left hand of the woman, and not on the right hand as has been continued for many hundreds of years." Certainly some fashionable ladies in the sixteenth and seventeenth centuries took to wearing their wedding rings upon their thumbs. In Thomas Southerne's play *Maid's Last Prayer*, of 1693, Lady Susan Malepert says, "Marry him I must, and wear my wedding ring upon my thumb too, that I am resolved on." However, this would seem to have been only a passing whim among the wealthy, and even these few moved their wedding rings to their thumbs only after the ceremony, during which they had the ring placed on the same finger as their less smart sisters.

Early writers on the subject of weddings, being almost entirely male, stress the left hand as the most suitable for the ring because it symbolizes the subjection of womankind. The right hand is masculine; man is the master. The left hand is feminine; woman is man's slave. In story and myth, the right hand has always stood for dominance, the left hand for submission and deviousness. The fourth finger, alone of all fingers, cannot be moved independently of its fellows. To lift it, one of the other fingers must be raised. Thus it always has a measure of additional protection. Another popular belief, held over many centuries, was that a vein or nerve ran straight from the heart to the fourth finger of the left hand.

St. Isidore of Seville taught, in the sixth century, that the groom gave his bride a ring as a sign of mutual love and placed it upon the fourth finger because a certain vein of blood ran straight to it from the heart, thus bringing about a peculiar intimacy and sympathy between that finger and the seat of affections. St. Isidore was not putting forward a new idea. He had picked up the notion from the Alexandrian historian, Appian, who had recorded the belief of ancient Egyptian anatomists that a certain delicate nerve passed from the fourth finger to the heart. This belief, starting with the Egyptians, spread with Christianity to almost every civilized country. It received the strong backing of the noted scientist and physician Laevinus Lemnius, who practiced in the

Low Countries and who died in 1568. In his treatise *De Occultis Naturae Miraculis*, published in English at Oxford in 1587, he scoffed at the idea of a nerve connection and stated that the link between the heart and the fourth finger was in fact made by a minute artery. In the case of a woman, the pulsations of this artery could be used to judge to what degree she was stimulated by an item of exciting intelligence. Lemnius used the direct connection to the heart afforded by this artery to effect cures. In his treatise he described how. "The small artery," he says, "is stretched forth from heart unto this finger, the motion whereof you may perceive evidently in all that affects the heart in women, by the touch of your forefinger. I used to raise such as were fallen into a swoon by pinching this joint, and by rubbing the ring of gold with a little saffron, for, by this, a restoring force that is in it passeth to the heart and refresheth the fountain of life unto which this finger is joined. Wherefore antiquity thought fit to compass it about with gold."

Although it is usual in contemporary western marriages for the wedding ring to be placed directly upon the fourth finger of the left hand during the service, it was not always so. Up to and in the sixteenth century the ring was moved in time to the invoking of the Trinity. At the words "In the name of the Father" the ring was placed on top of the thumb. On saying "In the name of the Son" the groom moved the ring to the top of the forefinger, then to the top of the middle finger on saying "and of the Holy Ghost." Finally the ring was put, and left in place, on the fourth finger on the closing word "Amen."

Given its symbolic importance, there is a superstitious reluctance to remove the wedding ring once it has been put in place, but it cannot always have held good for there used to be a common custom of passing pieces of wedding cake through the wedding ring during the reception. Lady Alice Houblon in her account *The Houblon Family* tells of an English wedding that took place in 1770. It was recorded step by step by the officiating parson, the Rev. Stotherd Abdy, whose narrative of the reception includes this passage:

> The Bride and Bridegroom's healths were drank and pieces of cake were drawn properly thro' the Wedding Ring for the dreaming Emolument of many spinsters and Batchelors.

The pieces of cake were passed through the ring a magical number of times, usually three, seven or nine times, wrapped in paper or a piece of linen, and placed beneath the pillow of a spinster or bachelor. Dreams of the future marriage partner were then supposed to follow. It was probably this custom that led to the present-day practice of sending out small boxes of wedding cake via the mail to those friends and relatives who could not attend the actual wedding ceremony. The combination of commercially baked wedding cake and slow postal services usually brings about a degree of staleness in the small piece of cake received that would make sleeping on it a much better bet than eating it. The custom, superstition or what you will was nicely expressed in *The Progress of Matrimony*, published in 1733.

> *But, madam, as a present take,*
> *This little paper of bride-cake;*
> *Fast any Friday in the year,*
> *When Venus mounts the starry sphere,*
> *Thrust this at night in pillow beer;*
> *In morning slumber you will seem*
> *T'enjoy your lover in a dream.*

The wedding cake has been a part of wedding ceremonies even longer than the wedding ring. While the ring symbolized the unity of the pair the cake looked to future fecundity, because cakes contain ground wheat flour, or that of some other corn, symbol of fertility and the earth's plenty. Today's wedding cake is generally supposed to be in direct line of descent from the Roman cake that formed an essential part of the patricians' wedding ceremony known as *confarreatio*. Here a simple wheat cake or biscuit was baked and broken, and the first morsels were eaten by the bride and groom. Then the remainder of the cake was broken over the bride's head, and the guests gathered up and devoured the crumbs. This was first a fertility rite, supposedly guaranteeing all concerned a life of plenty, blessed with children. Secondly, it formed the actual ceremony of marriage. It had to be performed in front of at least ten witnesses and was the only form of marriage that permitted the children arising from it to hold the highest sacred offices in the Roman community. Whether the wedding cake of today descended entirely from this Roman rite is by no means certain, however, for many other people throughout the world, who could not possibly have come under Roman influence, have similar ceremonies. In Sir John Lubbock's *Origin of Civilization* he tells us that his investigations have shown that "among the Iroquois, the bride and bridegroom used to partake together of a cake of 'sagamite' which the bride offered to the husband. The Fiji islanders have a very similar custom."

Among the Anglo-Saxon population of Britain they first threw

48

AN EXTRAORDINARY PIE

Here is a seventeenth-century English recipe for a "Bride Pye," which actually consisted of several pies, one inside another, each with its own filling.
(Robert May, 1660).

To make an extraordinary Pie, or a Bride Pye, of severall Compounds, being several different Pies on one bottom: Provide cocks-stones and combs, or lamb-stones and sweetbreads of veal, a little set in hot water and cut to pieces; also two or three ox-pallets blanched and slic't; a pint of oysters, sliced dates, a handful of pine kernels, a little quantity of broom-buds pickled, some fine interlarded bacon sliced, nine or ten chestnuts roasted and blanched, season them with salt, nutmeg, and some large mace, and close it up with some butter. For the caudle, beat up some butter, with three yolks of eggs, some white or claret wine, the juyce of a lemon or two; cut up the lid, pour on the lear, shaking it well together; then lay the meat, slic't lemon, and pickled barberries, and cov again, let these ingredients be put into the moddle or the lops of the Pie Several other Pies belong to the first form, but you be sure to make the three fashions proportionably answering one the other, you may set them on one bottom paste, which eill be more convenient; or if you set several you may bake the middle one full of flour, it be baked and cold,

take out the flour in the bottom, and in live birds, or a snake, which will seem strange to the beholders, which cut up the pie at the Table. This is for a Wedding to pass away time.

Now for the other Pies you may fill them with several ingredients, as in one you may put oysters, being parboiled and bearded, season them with large mace, pepper, beaten ginger, and salt, season them lightly and fill Pie, then lay on marrow and some good butter, close and bake it. Then make a lear of it with white-wine, oister liquor, three of four oisters bruised in pieces to it stronger, but take out the pieces, and an onion, on the bottom of the dish with a clove of garlick; it boild, put in a piece of butter, with a lemon, sweet will be good boild in it, bound up, fast together, cutt lid, or make a hole to let the lear in, &c.

Another you may make of prawns and cockles, seasoned as the first, but no marrow: a few pickled mushrooms, (if you have them) it being baked, heat piece of butter, a little vinegar, a slic't nutmeg, and juyce of two or three oranges thick, an pour it into the Pie.

wheat at the head of the bride, in addition to which she carried wheat stalks in her hand. Here again the wheat was picked up from the floor and eaten by the guests so it is not surprising that some early gourmet decided to upstage the other members of the community by baking the wheat into cake or biscuit form. These large, dry, flat discs were broken over the bride's head, and a similar custom continued in Scotland until the end of the nineteenth century and possibly later.

During the Tudor period the wedding biscuit began to reflect the greater sophistication of the times and became a wedding bun, small and rectangular. It was made of flour, sugar, egg, milk, spices and currants. These were baked and provided in very large numbers, not only by the families of the bride and groom but also by the guests. Some were still thrown over the bride, as she crossed the threshold of the house where the reception was being held, some were passed through the wedding ring to act as fortune tellers for the local spinsters and bachelors, and some were given to the poor. But the majority were piled up to form a centerpiece at the wedding feast. Thomas Deloney, in his *The Pleasant History of John Winchcomb*, describes a wedding procession in the time of Henry VIII:

49

Then there was a fair bride cup of silver and gilt carried before her (the bride) wherein was a goodly branch of Rosemarie gilded very faire hung about with silken ribands of all colors: next was there a noyse of musicians that played all the way before her: after her came all the chiefest maidens of the Countrie, some bearing great bride cakes and some Garlands of Wheate finely gilded and to the path unto the Church.

The wedding cake underwent another change in the next century. At the Restoration, King Charles II brought with him from France his own French chefs, for though glad to be restored to the English throne he was not at all enthusiastic about being restored to the mercy of the English cook. One of the culinary changes the French influence brought about was the icing of the wedding cake. Cakes rather, for at first the icing was placed as an outer casing around the pile of wedding-buns while the top was decorated with symbols associated with marriage. This arrangement made it easy to continue the custom of breaking the confection over the bride's head and even after the many buns had been replaced by the solid cake we know today, decorated with icing and marzipan, it continued to be torn up and poured over the bride—although some economy-minded or fashion-minded mothers used to provide two wedding cakes, one, small, to be torn and scattered: one, large and very decorative, to form the center piece of the wedding breakfast.

As weddings became more concerned with making a fashionable show the wedding cake began to be the concern of the professional confectioner rather than of the bride's mother or of the guests. Ann Monsarrat in her excellent book *And the Bride Wore . . .* gives some details of top weddings in America during the nineteenth century. "In October 1874, when the guests filed into the Chicago dining room of Mr. Henry Hamilton Honore, following the marriage of his daughter to young Colonel Frederick Grant (eldest son of President Ulysses S. Grant), they found at one end of the fourteen-foot table a 'Bride's Cake decorated with natural flowers,' and at the other end a 'Groom's Cake decorated with natural flowers'—and as the lilac-colored menus also informed them, these were supplemented by stewed terrapin, escalloped oysters, sweetbread, turkey and oyster patties, chicken and lobster salads, fillet of snipes 'in paper cases,' boned quail and boned prairie chicken, both 'in jelly form,' plus a multitude of other cakes, ices, meringues, wine jellies, fresh fruit and fruit salad; and, to see it all smoothly digested, tea, coffee and that king of champagnes, Krug." Later, Mrs. Monsarrat reports that, "In America in 1820, Louisa Quincy Adams, wife of the then Secretary of State, complained after the wedding of President Monroe's daughter: 'I didn't get a bit of cake and Mary had none to dream on.'" Eight years later, when John Quincy Adams was President and "Mary" (Mrs. Adams's niece) had grown old enough—and beautiful enough—to stir all three Adams boys into a fine romantic uproar, Mrs. Adams was again concerned with wedding cake. On February 26, 1828, she wrote to her youngest son (who had been first engaged to then discarded by the troublesome Mary) to tell him that his ex-fiancée had finally married his older brother and nothing but more misery could be foreseen. It was the day after the White House wedding and she explained: ". . . I am not much in a humor to write. I shall therefore only announce to you the fact that the wedding is over, that Madame is cool and easy and indifferent as ever and that John looks already as if he had all the cares in the world upon his shoulders . . . I send you a piece of cake as it is the fashion. Judge Cranch declined taking any as he said old people had nothing but dreams on such occasions."

The fashion for ostentatious wedding cakes was not confined to the United States. In England, at least two London firms were so prestigious that their names as cake makers were often printed in newspaper accounts of fashionable weddings, but the Rolls-Royce of wedding cakes were those supplied by Messrs. Bolland and Sons. One of the most elegant wedding cakes produced by this firm was presented by them to Princess Louise, Queen Victoria's fourth daughter, when she married the Marquis of Lorne in 1871. As described in the *Illustrated London News* the cake was

in three tiers, placed on a gold stand, weighing about 2 cwt., [224 lb.] and measuring at the base of the lower cake 2 ft. in diameter, and in height nearly 5 ft. The gold plateau had the Royal Arms at four equal distances, with cupids and flowers. The lower tier was ornamented with blue panels, baskets of flowers, fruit and love-birds between a scroll leaf, and medallions containing likenesses of the Marquis of Lorne and Princess Louise, with their respective coronets above. The second tier was festooned with rose, shamrock and thistle. The third tier was entirely of network, with cornucopias and shields on which were the monograms of the bride and bridegroom. The whole was surmounted by a handsome vase of flowers, with silk banners edged with silver fringe, containing the

Cakes by "Mr. Bolland of Chester." In Victorian England confectioners became architects as the cakes for society weddings became ever more massive and baroque.

armorial bearings of the Princess and of the Marquis. Each tier of the cake was bordered with trellis work studded with pearls.

In 1947, when Princess Elizabeth (later to become Queen Elizabeth II) married the Duke of Edinburgh, the *Illustrated London News* did not fail to include a description of the cake in its account of the ceremony.

The cake, 9 ft. high and weighing 500 lb., was made with four tiers, supported by silver pillars, and decorated with the armorial bearings of Princess Elizabeth and Lieutenant Philip Mountbatten, R.N.; plaques modelled in sugar depicting Buckingham Palace, Windsor Castle and Balmoral; figures illustrating the sporting activities and interests of the bride and bridegroom; the crests of the Royal Navy and Grenadier Guards; the badges of the A.T.S., the Girl Guides and the Sea Rangers; and shields bearing monograms of the bridal couple.

However elaborate the royal cake it was no doubt matched by an equally expansive and expensive wedding breakfast. Whether Duke and Princess or hardware clerk and typist, setting up in life together has always been an expensive business. Two may be able to live as cheaply as one in the land of proverbs but it rarely seems possible in real life, and couples today rely on the gifts presented at their wedding receptions and bridal showers. This fact was realized by our ancestors and sensibly allowed for at all levels of society. In his *Golden Grove Moralized*, published in 1608, William Vaughan wrote: "The marriage-day being come (in some shires of England), the invited guests do assemble together, and at the very instant of the marriage doe cast their presents (which they bestowe upon the new married folkes) into a bason, dish or cup, which standeth upon the table in the church, ready prepared for that purpose. But this manner is onely put in use amongst them which stand in need." Among the wealthier classes, gifts of money were regarded as being somewhat vulgar and costly articles were given as wedding presents instead. When Sir Philip Herbert married his Lady Susan in James I's reign, the gifts of plate and other items showered upon her were valued at £2,500, a vast sum at that time. Only the king's gift of £500, being a bridal portion, was in cash.

The poor, being of necessity more practical, still liked to receive cash on their wedding day, and so began the practice of holding a bride-ale in the church or, after the Reformation, in the church hall nearby. Following the wedding ceremony, a party would be held with food and drink being provided by the parents and friends of the married couple. Anyone who wanted could attend provided he or she could pay the sum fixed as an entrance fee. The sports which followed the feast were so designed as to draw still more money from the pockets of the participants into the ever-open purse of the newly-weds. If the bride-ale was held in a private house, the event was advertised by the hanging of a bush or branch out over the door in the same way that an inn advertised for trade. These were known as bride-stakes or bride-bushes.

Obviously these "open house" wedding receptions used to become pretty rowdy, for in Queen Elizabeth's day one English borough issued a by-law regulating the amount of beer that could be brewed for such a celebration and limiting the number of people who could attend to thirty-two.

Despite official disapproval the custom continued, and by the end of the eighteenth century the more enterprising couples were using the newspapers to try and draw in as many paying guests as possible.

Typical of these advertisements is the one that appeared in a newspaper in northwest England when George Hayto called upon all to join him in bringing home his bride, "Anne, the daughter of Joseph and Dinah Colin, on Thursday, the 7th day of May next" (1789). George's advertisement said that he would:

... be happy to see his friends and well-wishers; for whose amusement there will be a variety of races, wrestling matches, etc., etc. The prizes will be, a saddle, two bridles, a pair of "gands d'amour," gloves, which, whoever wins, is sure to marry within the twelve months; a girdle ("Ceinture de Venus") possessing qualities not to be described; and many other articles, sports and pastimes, too numerous to mention, but which can never prove tedious in the exhibition.

It would seem a pity that George Hayto was born before the establishment of the advertising business; he would seem to have had the natural touch.

Another young man with a gift for promotion was one Matthew Dawson, who placed the following advertisement in *Bell's Weekly Messenger*.

Matthew Dawson of Bothwell, Cumberland, intends to be married at Hohm Church, on the Thursday before Whitsuntide next, whenever that may happen, and to return to Bothwell to dine. Mr. Reid gives a Turkey to be roasted; Ed. Clementson gives a fat lamb to be roasted; Jos. Gibson gives a fat calf to be roasted. And in order that all this meat may be well basted, do you see Mary Pearson, Betty Hodgson, Mary Bushley, Molly Fisher, Sarah Briscre and Betty Porthouse give, each of them, a pound of butter. The advertiser will provide everything else for so festive an occasion. And he hereby gives notice, to all young women desirous of changing his condition, that he is at present disengaged; and advises them to consider, that, altho there be luck in leisure, yet, in this case, delays are dangerous; for, with him, he is determined it shall be first come first served.

Having made sure of drawing a large, paying, crowd to his wedding and subsequent bride-ale, the cunning Matthew Dawson made certain that the "first come" to Hohm Church was the young lady he had always intended to marry.

Matthew Dawson's bride may have worn white but it is by no

An invitation to a "bidding," Wales, 1861.
The value of gifts would be noted, and their donors would
receive gifts of equal value on similar occasions in the future.

means certain. It was not until the sixteenth century that the bride was expected to do so. Before then, and in many instances for a long time afterwards, the bride wore her very best dress. Clothes were extremely expensive and the idea of having a dress especially made for a wedding would have seemed madly extravagant. In many cases the bride's best dress would have been white anyway, for it was the color associated with virginity and purity and therefore very suitable for an unsullied maiden.

The bride in earlier days was distinguished from her unmarried contemporaries by three ornaments which no spinster could wear. These were the ring on her finger, the brooch on her breast and the garland on

55

her head. The brooch signified maidenly innocence and the garland, which typified the happiness and dignity of wedlock, was seen as the crown of victory accorded to her for subduing the temptations to evil that had beset her on her virtuous course from childhood to matrimony. In the eastern churches it was blessed by the officiating priest. This does not appear ever to have been the custom in the West but certainly the brides of medieval England were encouraged by their priests to regard the wearing of their garland as a privilege.

The crown or garland was made in many ways. Jeaffreson, in his *Brides and Bridals*, tells us that "in lands abounding with myrtle and olive, it was ordinarily composed of the leaves of those plants, intermixed with white and purple blossoms,—the white flowers being held to signify the innocence of girlhood, while the purple were symbolical of the Saviour's blood. In England roses and sprigs of myrtle were for a long period its principal materials . . . the leaves and blossoms were frequently fitted on a circlet of metal. Sometimes the flowers and sprigs were dispensed with and the bride was crowned with a hoop of golden appearance. . . . In several parts of the country it was the custom for the clergy and wardens of parish churches to provide coronets of metal or some other durable material for the ceremonious crowning of newly married women. Thus, the considerable sum of £3.10s was paid in 1560 to Alice Lewis, a goldsmith's wife, 'for a serclett to marry maidens in' by the wardens of St. Margaret's, Westminster. No particulars of the design of this head-ornament have been preserved, but it was probably composed of a gilt frame, supporting artificial flowers and ears of bearded wheat richly gilt. . . . A bride who brought her husband no money was in old times described as bringing him a chaplet of roses; and, in France, a father, unable to give his daughter any considerable pecuniary endowment on her wedding, used formally to tell her suitors that her fortune would be a garland."

There is uncertainty as to how the veil became part of the wedding ceremony. Historians have looked back to the bridal canopy of the Jews or the veil of the ancient Roman wedding ceremony, and some have even seen it as being symbolic of the flowing hair of the medieval bride or of the care-cloth that enveloped both the bride and groom at the Anglo-Saxon's marriage. All pleasant theories and some quite sensible. Certainly many people throughout the world sought to hide the bride from the envious and destructive eyes of the evil ones by disguising her or by veiling her from view. However, the bridal veil has played so little part in the English, and American, wedding since the early Anglo-Saxon days that it cannot properly be regarded as being traditional at all. It is in fact an item that appeared as a result of the fashion of the day being adopted by contemporary brides and then becoming accepted as a continuing integral part of a Western bride's dress. They appear to have become fairly general in the 1840s but obviously were still unusual enough to call for comment outside the most fashionable circles in 1854. It was on February 7 of that year that the Reverend Mr. Armstrong, an English country vicar, wrote in his diary: "A day of excitement in the parish in consequence of Miss Dringle's wedding and her wearing a veil, supposed to be the first ever seen in Dereham." In her book *Two Centuries of Costume in America* Mrs. Alice Morse Earle wrote, in 1903: "The earliest wedding-veil and all-white bridal gown made distinctly for a wedding-dress, which I have known was worn by Mrs. James H. Heyward, of Charleston, South Carolina. She was Decima Cecilia Shubrich, a lovely creature, who married at nineteen . . . in the year 1800. [In her portrait] she wears a tulle wedding veil placed on the head as would be a similar bridal veil today."

Another comparatively late introduction into England and America was the now ubiquitous orange-blossom. It is said that the Moors first introduced the orange tree into Spain. There it was a rarity and much prized. A story is told of how the King of Spain's tree was coveted by the French ambassador. He knew that the gardener's daughter longed to marry but could not because she had no dowry. The ambassador approached her and offered her a generous dowry in return for a cutting from the precious orange tree. She eagerly fell in with his plan, secured the cutting undetected and was able to marry her lover. On her wedding day, wishing to honor the tree that had brought her happiness, she wove a circlet of orange-blossom and wore it in her raven hair. Be that as it may, there is no doubt that the custom of weaving a bouquet or circlet of orange-blossom for wearing on the wedding day passed from Spain to France, from France to England, in about 1820, and from there to America where it was worn at a White House wedding by Mary Hellen, who married the son of President John Quincy Adams in 1828.

The symbolism of orange-blossom is said to be one of virginity and the promise of fecundity. The white blossoms are the symbol of innocence and purity but the orange tree has the reputation of bearing a superabundance of fruit and so the bride who wears it can hope to acquire a similar fruitfulness. This regrettably sexy image gave offense to one Victorian commentator who wrote that:

In England tradition still holds that good luck will befall the bride who has been kissed by a chimney sweep.

It would be as well, perhaps, if our brides would revive the practice of English womankind in former days, and brighten their wreaths with green, purple, red and crimson. The large, colorless crown never brightens, usually lowers, the effects of a bride's beauty. Not one lovely girl in a thousand can wear it without disadvantage to her good looks. Custom and romance have raised the chaplet of orange-blossoms to unmerited respect. The white of the orange-flower is an impure white, and the symbolism of the plant is a reason why some other flower should be adopted by the English bride.

Perhaps modern brides should return to the wearing of rosemary. In a wedding sermon given in 1607, Roger Hackett, Doctor of Divinity, said: "Let this Ros Marinus—the flower of men, ensigne of your wisdome, love and loyaltie—be carried, not only in your hands, but in your heads and hearts."

1770s

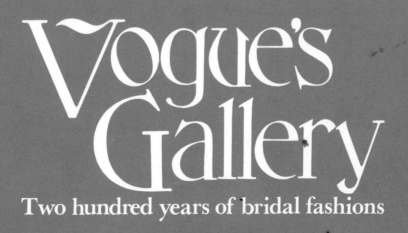

Vogue's Gallery

Two hundred years of bridal fashions

1800s

1830s

1860s

1850s

1860s

1870s

flowers

train

1930s

SACRED AND PROFANE

"To church the parties went,
At once with carnal and devout intent" ALEXANDER POPE

DURING THE PERIOD when the Puritans were in power in England and royalty was "away" in Europe, the observances of religion reached a peak of public obedience that has only been matched by life under the Catholic Queen Mary. Surprisingly this was the period when marriage moved, officially, furthest away from the Church. The Puritans saw the Anglican Book of Common Prayer, its wedding service and the "devil's circlet"—the wedding ring—as popish and idolatrous. To replace them, they instituted a mode of civil marriage which was made law on September 29, 1653. Now couples wishing to marry had to state their intention to the parish registrar and give him all their personal details. The registrar would then publish the banns on three separate occasions: either on Sundays in their church or in the market place on market day. Once this had been done, the registrar issued a certificate to the couple who then were married before a justice of the peace after joining hands and exchanging binding promises. No attempt was made, however, to prevent the couple having their marriage blessed by a clergyman either before or after the civil ceremony. Generally a service of blessing was held in church according to the form laid down in the *Directory of Public Worship* which had been written to replace the Book of Common Prayer.

The wedding service laid down by the *Directory* consisted of a solemn prayer by the officiating minister, an extempore declaration made by the same person of the ends of marriage, and an exhortation to the bride and bridegroom followed by the joining of hands, without the use of the ring, and an exchange of promises. Says the *Directory*:

After solemn charging of the persons to be married, before the great God, who searcheth all hearts, and to whom they must give a strict account at the last day, that if either of them know any cause, by precontact or otherwise, why they may not lawfully proceed to marriage, that they now discover it: the minister (if no impediment be acknowledged) shall cause, first, the man to take the woman by the right hand, saying these words: "I, 'M,' doe take thee 'N,' to be my married wife, and doe in the presence of God, and before this congregation, promise and covenant to be a loving and faithful husband unto thee, until God shall separate us by death." Then the woman shall take the man by the right hand and say these words: "I, 'N,' doe take thee, 'M,' to be my married husband, and I doe, in the presence of God, and before this congregation, promise and covenant to be a loving, faithful and obedient wife unto thee, until God shall separate us by death." Then, without any further ceremony, the minister shall, in the face of the congregation, pronounce them to be husband and wife, according to God's ordinance; and so conclude the action with prayer to this effect.

The necessity for a civil marriage only stood until Cromwell became Lord Protector. In 1656, his parliament confirmed the previous marriage law but did not confirm the vital clause that had stated "that no other marriage whatsoever within the Commonwealth of England shall be held or accounted a legal marriage." Despite the fact that a wedding celebrated solely in church was now not illegal, many people continued to play safe and have two ceremonies, one before a justice of the peace and one before a minister of the church.

Not surprisingly, the Puritan pilgrims who went to America carried their views on the way weddings should be celebrated with them, not only to New England but even into that royalist and reactionary stronghold, Virginia. In the middle of the seventeenth century, Virginian magistrates were empowered to conduct weddings and, rather than have the banns read out in church, the couple could just nail a notice to the church door. The cost of a wedding license signed by the governor in 1672 was 100 pounds of tobacco, Virginia's most popular currency, while the price of having your banns read in church was forty pounds of tobacco. Weddings in New York State could also be performed solely before a magistrate, a fact that shocked a visiting English clergyman in 1695.

The transference of weddings from priest to magistrate and of the calling of the banns from church to market place did not escape the attention of the humorists of the time. One wondered that as marriage and hanging were supposed to be predestined, then who better to supervise weddings than those who ordered executions? Along the same lines another witty fellow highlighted the similarly fatal longterm effects for a man on being fitted either with a rope around his neck or with the manacles of wedlock. Richard Flecknoe, trying to make a genuine point through light verse, published a long poem in 1656, "On the Justices of Peace's making Marriages and crying them in the Market." Two verses make his point well:

> *Let parson and vicar then say what they will,*
> *The custom is good (God continue it still);*
> *For marriage being now a traffique and trade,*
> *Pray, where but in markets should it be made?*
>
> *'Twas well ordained they should be no more,*
> *In churches or chapels, then, as before;*
> *Since for in Scripture, we have an example,*
> *How buyers and sellers were driven out o' the Temple.*

When royalty returned to the throne of England, in the person of Charles II, the justices of the peace were relieved of their wedding duties and could concentrate once again on upholding the law. Lest those who had been married by them during the king's absence should be worried about the legality of their position, which they had no reason to be, a legislative enactment was passed which declared the validity of all marriages by justices of the peace since May 1, 1642. This no doubt gave comfort to many ignorant of the fact, as were obviously Charles's lawmakers, that civil marriage was legal in England and always had been and that no blessing by the Church was actually called for.

Some muddled thinking on the matter is, perhaps, not surprising as England had a long history of religious differences—between Catholicism and Nonconformism, between Catholicism and the episcopal Church of England and between the Church of England and Nonconformism. Whoever was in power tended to lay down one law, while the suppressed parties continued to be married in secret according to their own custom. All this clandestine marrying established a feeling for secret weddings that ran through English society for a large part of the seventeenth and eighteenth centuries. Another factor that made a very positive contribution to this custom was that of down-to-earth economy. For a middle-class or an upper-class family a public wedding had to be an occasion for very obvious spending. Father had to show the neighbors and all the family's wide circle of friends and acquaintances that he was a man of substance who could send off his daughter in style. It took a man of very strong character to do otherwise. One such was Sir William Penn, father of the founder of Pennsylvania, a neighbor of the diarist Samuel Pepys and his colleague at the Admiralty. He shocked and annoyed Pepys, who did not like to miss any possible occasion for jollification, by marrying his daughter off publicly but quietly. On February 15, 1667, Pepys noted in his diary: "Home and to dinner, where I hear Pegg Penn is married this day privately; no friends, but two or three relations on his side and hers. Borrowed many things of my kitchen for dressing their dinner." He was told that the wedding was private because it was just before Lent. "... and so in vain to make new clothes till Easter, that they might see the fashions as they are like to be this summer; which is reason and good enough. Mrs. Turner tells me that she hears he gives £4,500 or £4,000 with her. They are gone to bed, so I wish them much sport."

Five days later, Pepys noted, "His wedding hath been so poorly kept, that I am ashamed of it; for a fellow that makes such a flutter as he do." Two days after that Pepys and his wife were asked to dinner by the Penns but even this did not make the diarist any better pleased with the whole affair. "It is instead of a wedding dinner for his daughter, whom I saw in palterly clothes, nothing new but a bracelet that her husband had given her, and ugly she is, as heart can wish. A sorry dinner, not anything handsome or clean, but some silver plates they borrowed of me . . . home to supper and to bed, talking with my wife of the poorness and meanness of all that Sir W. Penn and the people about us do . . . ."

With friends and neighbors reacting in that way to a quiet wedding, it is hardly surprising that many fathers tended to encourage their daughter's romantic inclinations for a "secret" wedding. Knowing that her father approved, privately, a daughter could "elope," have a secret wedding ceremony and then return home to his public forgiveness and personal congratulations. The bride had a romantic experience, the father was saved a fortune and the groom gained some of the money not wasted on clothes and entertainment in the form of a larger dowry.

Toward the end of the seventeenth century a French protestant, Maximilian Misson, took refuge in England. He found a position as tutor to the Duke of Ormonde's grandson and looked around at English society with all the interest of a space traveler newly arrived on an inhabited planet. In his journal *Memoirs and Observation in his Travels over England* he recorded the curious ways of the English.

One of the reasons that they have for marrying secretly, as they generally do in England, is that thereby they avoid a great deal of expense and trouble. . . . Persons of quality, and many others who imitate them, have lately taken up the custom of being married very late at night in their chamber, and very often at some country house. . . . The bridegroom, that is to say the husband that is to be, and the bride, that is the wife who is to be, conducted by their father and mother, or those that serve them in their room, and accompany'd among others by two bridemen and two bridesmaids, with a licence in their pocket, call up Mr. Curate and his clerk, and tell him their business; are marry'd with a low voice and the door shut; tip the minister a guinea and the clerk a crown; steal softly out, one one way and t'other another, either on foot or in coaches, go different ways to some tavern, at a distance from their own lodgings, or to the house of some trusty friends, there have a good dinner, and return home at night as quietly as lambs."

The use of a license obviated the necessity of having the banns publicly called and enabled the happy pair to keep the whole affair very dark. Unless of course, as quite often happened, the clerk had an arrangement with one of the local butchers' groups who formed marrowbone and cleaver bands, producing their "music" by clashing the meat bones and their axes together. Tipped off by the clerk, or some other informant at church or inn, the butchers' band would assemble under the happy couple's window at daybreak and make their hideous music until the bridegroom paid enough to persuade them to give up and go away.

The secret marriage and the use of a very expensive special license was by no means confined to England alone. American society adopted the practice as well and in New York State it was considered very ungenteel to have your banns called in church. In 1765 delays in the shipping from England had caused a shortage of the official stamped license forms that were normally signed by the governor. For a brief period it became fashionable to have the banns called in church and the press and responsible opinion generally welcomed this return to good sense and respectability, predicting that this new fashion had come to stay. Alas, once the ship arrived and the officially stamped special licenses could once again be signed by the governor, back came the secret weddings among fashionable New York society.

With middle- and upper-class weddings being conducted as stealthily as burglaries in England, it is perhaps not surprising that they became closely associated with prisons and convicted criminals. The

A Fleet marriage certificate, 1727. The couple were married at one of the several "Hand and Pen"
taverns surrounding the Fleet.

notorious Fleet Prison in London was a place where people who could
not pay their debts were sent until they had discharged them. In the
period between the Restoration and the death of George II, the
population of the Fleet was usually around 600 people of both sexes, but
only about a third of this number, usually the poorest, lived inside the
walls of the prison as true captives. The remainder, provided they could
pay a hefty sum to the Warden of the Fleet and also give sureties against
their decamping for good, were allowed to live in rooms or inns outside
the walls of the prison within what were known as the "rules" or the
"liberties" of the Fleet. These were within the immediate neighborhood

of the prison and formed a raffish area with an atmosphere all its own. The prisoner enjoying the "liberties" had to report daily to the porter of his "college" and if the warders or constables of the Fleet believed that a prisoner was likely to break his parole then they would summarily curtail the bail and the prisoner would be back inside again.

The district around the Fleet Prison had inns of every quality and many skittle-yards and gambling establishments. The people who lived within the rules came from every social class but were likely to have certain things in common; openhandedness with money, even if it was someone else's, and a contempt for the rules of "respectable" society. It was a natural place, therefore, for the trade in cheap, secret weddings to flourish. People did not want to publish their banns and they did not, if possible, want to pay the tax imposed on special licenses. At the same time, respectable ministers who married a couple in church without banns or license were liable to a very heavy fine. But the law of the land, strictly interpreted, meant that a couple did not need either a license, a church or an ordained minister in order to be married. All that was required was a civil ceremony, a mutual contract, that could as easily be held in a tavern room or on a street corner as in a church. The number of discredited clergymen who lived within the rules around the Fleet saw this situation as an excellent way in which to gain some much needed extra food, drink and cash. The innkeepers of the area enthusiastically agreed with them. Together the priest and the publican would fit up a room in the tavern as a wedding "chapel" in which marriages could be celebrated by the priest and his "clerk," usually the publican himself. The wedding party could then do all its entertaining at the inn itself; most convenient and profitable to both entrepreneurs. Sometimes the priest kept all his fees and the innkeeper benefited from the appetites of the wedding party but often all the profits went to the publican who managed the whole affair himself and kept the priest on his payroll at an annual salary of some twenty pounds and board and lodging.

Not all of the Fleet parsons worked with or for innkeepers. Some of the less broken-down kept their own establishments and made everything look reasonably official. They maintained registers, kept accounts and now and again wrote down some of the more unusual happenings at these clandestine weddings:

June 10, 1729—John Nelson, of ye Parish of St. George, Hanover, bachelor and gardener, and Mary Barnes of ye same, sp. married. Cer. dated 5 November 1727, to please their parents.

Married at barber's shop one Kerrils, for half a guinea, after which it was extorted out of my pocket, and for fear of my life, delivered.

Competition between the Fleet parsons and their associated innkeepers was keen, and their touts combed the nearby streets looking for likely customers. It was assumed by them that every passing couple was there solely with matrimony in mind and they pressed the cause of their particular parson with vigor, fighting with one another over a likely looking pair of customers. A London newspaper dated May 29, 1736, gives a contemporary account.

Having frequently heard of the many abominable practices of the Fleet, I had the curiosity on Sunday, May 23rd, to take a view of the place as I was accidently passing by. The first thing I observed was one J—— L——, by trade a carpenter (whose brother it is said keeps the sign of the B—— and G——) cursing and swearing and raving in the streets, in the time of divine service, with a mob of people about him, calling one of his fraternity (J.E.), a plyer for weddings, an informing rogue, for informing against one of their ministers for profane cursing and swearing, for which he paid three pounds odd money. . . . When the riot was dispersed, I walked about some small time, and saw a person exceedingly well dressed in a flowered morning-gown, a band, hat and wig, who appeared so clean that I took him for some worthy divine who might accidentally have come out of the country, and as accidentally be making the same remarks with myself; but upon inquiry was surprised at being assured that he was one T—— C——, a watchmaker, who goes in minister's dress, personating a clergy-man, and taking upon him the name of Doctor, to the scandal of the sacred function. He may be seen at any time at the "Bull and Garter," or the great "Hand and Pen and Star," with these words written, "The Old and True Register," near the Rainbow Coffee House. Please to give this a place in your paper, and you will not only oblige one of your constant readers, but may prevent many innocent persons from being ruined.

The "Hand and Pen" became so famous as a marrying house that several competitors with the same name were set up.

But in 1754 the Lord Chancellor of England, Lord Hardwicke, had his Marriage Bill enacted. This required that marriages should be

71

solemnized with the publication of banns or licenses; that they should be solemnized in the parochial churches or chapels where "banns of matrimony had usually been published," and that any clergyman who ignored the new law should, on conviction, "be deemed and adjudged to be guilty of felony, and should be transported to some of His Majesty's plantations in America for the space of fourteen years." The bill was much opposed both within Parliament and without, but it became law except in Scotland and in the case of professing Jews and Quakers.

Although Lord Hardwicke's Act killed off the clandestine Fleet weddings in effect, it did not subdue the British urge to marry secretly, particularly when an unscrupulous adventurer was able to carry off some tender young heiress. Because Scotland had been exempted from the Marriage Act there was no need for banns, residence or indeed a genuine special license. This happy fact brought fame to Gretna Green, a little village just over the Scots border and easily accessible from England.

Despite popular belief, the runaway couples at Gretna Green were never married by a blacksmith. Few of the notorious "couplers," as they were called, were anything like so respectable as a worthy smith. The first person to take advantage of the change in English law was a man called Scott who lived in a cottage outside Gretna Green. He was followed by a retired soldier, one George Gordon, who always wore his somewhat tattered military uniform when carrying out his own version of the wedding service. This included a cocked hat, red coat, high boots and a ponderous sword of antique design. Like most old soldiers, George Gordon knew the value of official looking documents when trying to back up a rather thin story. Accordingly he used to brandish a torn parchment, which he claimed was a special commission from the government that gave him authority to conduct weddings. Few of his immediate cronies could read and in any case he never let anyone handle his "commission"; after all, he used to claim, it cost him fifty pounds a year and was far too valuable to let out of his charge.

With the aid of his fake parchment and old broadsword George Gordon joined in unholy matrimony many an eloping heiress and her smooth-talking abductor. It was a profitable business and it is not surprising that other enterprising rogues were determined to get in on the act. The most successful of these was Joe Paisley, once of the tobacco trade. He made a bow in the direction of the church by dressing as a parson in gown, cassock, bands and a three-cornered hat. His manner, too, was carefully clerical. At first, he used to join the hands of the happy pair together and call a blessing down upon them from heaven. Then he

A Gretna marriage certificate, 1819. The witnesses, both illiterate, were a postboy and a stableman.

would give them a marriage certificate of his own devising, and very eccentric spelling, which he signed with a variety of false names. He stopped doing this when he was advised by a lawyer that he was in danger of prosecution, and instead gave his clients a certificate signed in his real name certifying that he had personally witnessed them exchanging binding promises of marriage. In this way he broke no law, performed a welcome service and became wealthy enough to indulge his inordinate appetite for brandy.

The capturing and forcible marriage of heiresses by desperate young men short of ready money had always been a feature of English high-society life as can be seen by the legislation passed to prevent it in the reigns of Henry VII, Philip and Mary, Elizabeth I and George IV. Such legislation, although forceful in intention, appears to have done little to stop the really determined. Daniel Defoe, writing in 1727, says:

73

The arts and tricks made use of to trepan, and, as it were, kidnap young women away into the hands of brutes and sharpers, were very scandalous, and it became almost dangerous for anyone to leave a fortune to the disposal of the person that was to enjoy it; and where it was so left, the young lady went always in danger of her life; she was watched, laid wait for and, as it were, beseiged by a continual gang of rogues, cheats, gamesters and such like starving crew so that she was obliged to confine herself like a prisoner . . . or else she was snatched up, seized, hurry'd up into a coach-and-six, a fellow dressed up in a clergyman's habit to perform the ceremony, and a pistol clapt to her breast to make her consent to be marry'd, and thus the work was done.

Sometimes the approach to the heiress was made with less violence and more cunning. Early in the 1800s a group of English expatriates lived in Paris who prided themselves on their avant-garde views, smart appearance and fashionable ways. By the rather rigid standards of true English society they were not acceptable but by living in Paris and creating their own society they were able to pretend to a degree of aristocracy they did not possess, and all joined in preserving the charade. Two of the handsomest and cleverest members of this society were the brothers Edward and William Gibbon Wakefield. They were much in demand and entertained lavishly themselves. Sadly, their bankers became less and less ready to advance them further loans and so desperate remedies were called for.

Edward decided to steal away a young English heiress, fifteen-year-old Ellen Turner, only daughter of a wealthy manufacturer. He sent his valet to Ellen's school, where, with alarming but plausible tales of illness in the family, the headmistress was persuaded to let Ellen go home. Instead the girl found herself at Gretna Green, having been lured to the altar by Edward's lies. Her father, Edward told her, was bankrupt and had been arrested for debt at the Scottish border as he was on his way to join them. Edward was rich, and would lend Mr. Turner £60,000, asking only for interest at a trifling rate and Ellen's hand in marriage: he was, he claimed, in love with her. Further persuaded by a letter supposedly from her father's attorney calling upon her to "show the same fortitude that her father had evinced on the occasion of his losses," Ellen agreed to marry.

Mr. and Mrs. Wakefield left for France. At Calais, the kidnapper opened negotiations with Mr. Turner. He would return his wife to her parents upon receiving sworn assurances that they would pay him an annual allowance sufficient to enable him to live as one of the leading members of "the first Society in Europe." Though distressed, Mr. Turner did not fail to use that acumen which had made him wealthy. Pretending to fall in with Edward's wishes, he lured him back to England and had him arrested, tried and sentenced to three years in Newgate Prison. A special act of Parliament was passed which declared the marriage to be at an end. The affair was not without consequence in other spheres: while in prison, Edward Gibbon Wakefield prepared a book on capital punishment and began to formulate the ideas about emigration and settlement which were to make him famous as a strong colonial influence in Canada, Australia and New Zealand.

While marriages in England and Scotland seem to have revolved around heiresses and the world of fashion, life in America was much simpler. Life among the good people of Nantucket is well and lovingly described by J. Hector St. John de Crevecoeur, a member of the French nobility who chose to settle in the state of New York in 1769, where he married and became a farmer. His *Letters from an American Farmer* are a warm account of the people amongst whom he chose to live. Writing of the manners and customs at Nantucket, he observes:

Every man takes a wife as soon as he chooses, and that is generally very early; no portion is required, none is expected: no marriage articles are drawn up among us by skilful lawyers to puzzle and lead posterity to the bar or to satisfy the pride of the parties. We give nothing with our daughters; their education, their health, and the customary outset are all that the fathers of numerous families can afford.

This equable and virtuous pattern of marriage followed upon an equally decorous courtship as he later shows:

The young fellows . . . find out which is the most convenient house and there they assemble with the girls of the neighborhood. Instead of cards, musical instruments or songs, they relate stories of their whaling voyages, their various sea adventures and talk of the different coasts and people they have visited. "The Island of Catharine in Brazil," says one, "is a very droll island; it is inhabited by none but men; women are not permitted to come in sight of it; not a woman is there on the whole island. Who amongst

The wedding of George Washington, 1759. His bride was a widow distinguished for her wealth and beauty, Mrs. Martha Custis.

us is not glad it is not so here? The Nantucket girls and boys beat the world."

Thus these young people sit and talk and divert themselves as well as they can; if anyone had lately returned from a cruise, he is generally the speaker of the night; they often all laugh and talk together, but they are happy and would not exchange their pleasures for those of the most brilliant assemblies in Europe. This lasts until the father and mother return, when all retire to their respective homes, the men reconducting the partners of their affections. Thus they spend many of the youthful evenings of their lives; no wonder, therefore, that they marry so early.

Not all visitors from Europe saw such a good side of America. Peter Kalm, a young Swedish scientist who toured America in 1748, was saddened by the condition of the slaves.

It is greatly to be pitied that the masters of these Negroes take little care of their spiritual welfare . . . there are some who would be very ill-pleased and would in every way hinder their Negroes from being instructed in the doctrines of Christianity . . . partly through fear of the Negroes growing too proud on seeing themselves upon a level

A wedding between slaves belonging to a rich Brazilian household, early nineteenth century.

with their masters in religious matters. . . . To prevent any disagreeable mixtures of the white people and Negroes, and to hinder the latter from forming too great opinions of themselves, to the disadvantage of their masters, I am told there was a law passed prohibiting the whites of both sexes to marry Negroes, under pain of capital punishment, with deprivation of privileges and other, severer, penalties for the clergyman who married them. But that the whites and blacks sometimes copulated appears in children of a mixed complexion who are sometimes born. . . . At present Negroes are seldom brought to the English colonies, for those already there have multiplied rapidly. In regard to marriage they proceed as follows: in case you have not only male but likewise female Negroes, they may intermarry, and then the children are all your slaves. But if you possess a male only and he has an inclination to marry a female belonging to a different master, you do not hinder your Negro in so delicate a point; but it is of no advantage to you, for the children belong to the master of the female. Therefore it is in practice advantageous to have Negro women.

In 1804 some half a century after the above accounts were first

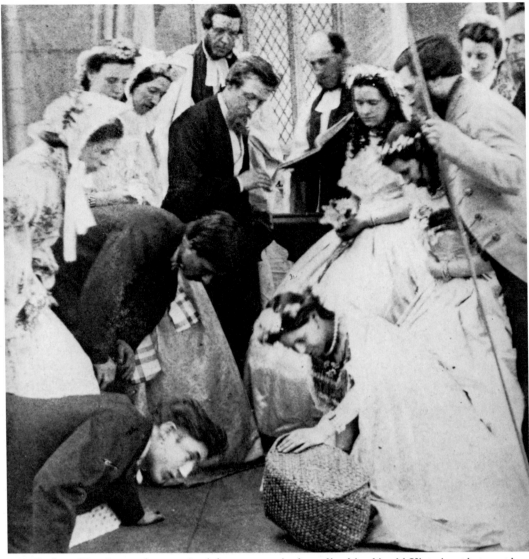

"The Lost Ring," every best man's nightmare amusingly realized in this old Victorian photograph.

published, a Miss Eliza Southgate Browne wrote of a New York wedding as follows: "Miss Pell was married last week to Robert MacComb; they are making a prodigious dash. I went to pay the bride a visit on Friday; they had an elegant ball and supper in the evening, as it was the last day of seeing company; seven bride's maids and seven bride men, most superb dresses; the bride's pearls cost 1,500 dollars; they spend the winter in Charleston."

Despite the influence of Puritanism, despite the restrictions imposed upon the new nation's slaves and the quiet simplicity of Nantucket's settlers, it is clear that America's upper classes were celebrating their weddings with all the opulence and splendor of their European cousins.

Here Comes The Bride

An album of wedding photographs

ABOVE *Two weddings of the European aristocracy, before and after World War I.*

MAIN PICTURE *Further down the social scale, but clearly having a better time, are these French villagers, 1908.*

The conclusion of a successful hunt, England 1907.

These photographs range from exotic British India (below far left) to the groom's backyard (left), from England in the 1860s (center far left) to Wisconsin in the 1930s (above).

Customs and curiosities in Britain and America with (right) a middle American group from the 1920s, (below) a tinker wedding on the Isle of Lewis, Scotland, (center right) the bride throwing her bouquet after her marriage in Cooperstown, New York in 1908, (far right) a Hollywood night club wedding in the 1940s, and (below far right) a country wedding in England in the 1870s.

THE EUROPEAN EXPERIENCE

"Notwithstanding all that wit, or malice, or pride, or prudence will be able to suggest, men and women must at last pass their lives together" DR. JOHNSON

AT THE UTTERMOST northern point of Europe live the Lapps, known to themselves as *Samek*. Traditionally they rely heavily upon their reindeer herds for survival among the ice and snow and gather together in large numbers once a year, usually in January or February, at large fairs where they can barter their products for the things they need to get them through yet another hard year. At these fairs they meet a wide selection of people from clans other than their own, and it is obviously a good time for young men to select a bride. They spend the first day or so looking at the young girls going about their chores and finally decide upon the one they think will make a good wife. Having decided, a boy will usually address a few decorous words to the girl of his choice, and her family will then wait for the boy to call. This he will do, pay the girl a formal compliment and sit down without invitation. Silence follows as the girl and her family sit gazing out of the tent flap into the middle distance. After a decent interval, the young man will ask if he can make coffee. The coffee pot and the cups are put before him, still without a word, and he brews and serves the coffee hopefully. For this is the testing time. If the parents drink the coffee and signify pleasure, then the suitor is accepted. If they ignore it all he can do is bow formally and withdraw, rejected. The drinking of the coffee is taken virtually as a binding engagement which will be marked by the young man giving the girl a ring. A few days later, at the wedding ceremony, the young couple will exchange rings in the presence of a pastor. Most Lapps are members of the strict Christian cult of Laestadism, though some belong to the Orthodox Church. The bride will now wear two rings, and she will add a third when her first male child is born. The ceremony will be followed by a feast at which almost all those present at the fair are welcome. A male relation will pass among the guests with a plate into which the guests drop money, and at the same time they will promise to give the couple a reindeer or a calf. These promises are carefully noted by yet another

86

relative and followed up so that the bride and groom start life with a fair-sized herd of their own when they set up together either in the tent of the wife's family or in their own tent alongside. It is in the mother that the Lapps see the essence of the family; she is the stabilizing influence and she produces the children who see to the continuance of the line and to the continued care of the reindeer herd when the parents get old.

The Lapps are very faithful one to another and divorce is almost unknown. In this they are unlike the society of neighboring Sweden. There, in the towns particularly, marriage is regarded as a voluntary form of cohabitation, and no legal or social barrier is put in the way of a couple wishing to separate. Indeed, young people very often move in together before they get married and quite often do not bother to go through a wedding ceremony at all. It is quite common for such couples to have children and nobody finds such behavior odd or immoral. About two thirds of all the known unmarried mothers live with the father of their child. Those who do not, receive a contribution from the father towards the child's upkeep. Should this not be forthcoming, the mother can obtain an agreed sum from the state which will, in turn, eventually recover it from the father.

Those who do want to get married can do so either at a civil ceremony or at a religious one. First, the young couple must apply to the authorities in the parish in which they are residing for their papers to be checked and for the girl to receive a certificate of *hindersprövning* showing that there is no impediment to the marriage. If they want a Swedish church wedding, then at least one of the couple must be a member of the established Church of Sweden. If they belong to another religion, they can be married in the church of the faith. For a civil marriage, the couple has to apply to the nearest *tingsrätt* or district court, which issues a marriage license after the ceremony which takes place before witnesses. The registrar will follow the laid-down form of service, and begin by saying: "The purpose of marriage is the welfare of the individual and the continuance of society. You have made known your desire to marry one another."

He will conclude: "Never forget the vow of faithfulness for life that you have now made. Live together in mutual respect, love and confidence, and remember your responsibility towards generations to come. May unanimity and happiness reign in your marriage and in your home."

This is sensible and practical advice, but a far cry from the days when each Swedish girl dreamed of becoming a virgin bride at Whitsun.

This feast day was originally celebrated as a spring festival, and a young virgin was chosen to go through a mock wedding ceremony in the cause of fertility, and in the hope of placating the natural forces. So holy were the couple as a result of this mock wedding that they were thought to be too pure for mere human contact and were doomed thereafter to live a. life of celibacy. Understandably, girls were reluctant to take the place of the real Whitsun bride but they believed they gained good fortune if they made their own marriages at that time. The church would be decorated with wild flowers from the meadows and a young tree, fresh from the forest, would be placed on each side of the altar. The bride, proud of her virginity, would wear white and a high-pointed crown. After the service there would be a feast and dancing and all the young men of the neighborhood would vie with each other to dance with the Queen of the Day. In the Swedish province of Blekinge they used to choose a Midsummer Bride, to whom the church wedding "coronet" would sometimes be lent. The girl chosen would select a bridegroom for herself and a collection would be made for the pair, who, for the time of the celebration, would be looked upon as man and wife.

A midsummer bride was also chosen by the people of southern Finland, who crowned the girl of their choice and danced with her all night long. The bridal crown was the most distinctive feature of the Finnish bride up until the 1920s. Generally it was cone-shaped but in the south of the country it was crescent-shaped, hung with trinkets. To add to her glory, the bride would borrow as much jewelry as she could for the great day. In most parishes there was an old woman who specialized in dressing the bride and who hired out bridal trinkets and crowns. The bride's dress would be largely the work of herself and her female relatives. She would have been preparing her trousseau from childhood, along with many other garments and items which formed part of her dowry. She was also expected to have made a variety of gifts, to be given out on the wedding day to her mother-in-law and to the men who had arranged the wedding. These gifts would take the form of gloves, stockings, ribbons, belts, shirts and other embroidered items.

The courtship followed the custom of "bundling" common in cold northern climates. The selected young man would be allowed to spend the night with the girl, in bed but not between the same layers of bedding. Whatever else he might be admiring during this time he would be expected to comment on the fine handiwork shown on the items of her dowry, which would be tastefully displayed around her bedroom.

Midsummer and Christmas were the most popular times for

Finnish weddings, Midsummer because of its old association with fertility and "life-renewal" ceremonies and Christmas because it was the time when all the harvests had been gathered in and when further work was difficult if not impossible. On the day of the wedding, the bride would go the sauna with her friends for a ritual bath and on her return home her hair would be unbraided and cut short whilst the older ladies of her household sobbed loudly to demonstrate their sorrow at losing a daughter from the house. Married women never displayed their hair, and after the cutting ceremony the girl would be presented with a *tzepy*, a linen cap of the sort she would wear constantly from that day forward. The bride would then be dressed in a fashionable dress with a hooped skirt and would have a traditional ornamented collar placed around her shoulders. From her belt would hang ribbons and upon her head was placed the ceremonial bride's crown. This has to be very firmly fixed: she sometimes had to wear it for as long as the celebrations lasted, up to three days on some occasions, which meant sleeping sitting up with her head supported. She could only hope that the young men who would aim to dance the crown off her head would succeed fairly early on. She could then put on her *tzepy* and relax.

After the bride was crowned she would kneel before her parents, who would signify their blessing by holding a loaf of bread over her head. After this she was formally presented to her groom, who would have arrived earlier at her parents' house. The wedding breakfast would then take place before the actual ceremony, the main dish usually being a nourishing stew brimming with meat and vegetables. Most Finns are members of the Lutheran Church, but in western Finland the Orthodox Church has many followers and it is here that the actual wedding ceremony is most colorful. In addition to the magnificently gowned priests, the exchange of crowns or wreaths and other ceremonies of the Orthodox wedding ceremony, the young couple used to stand beneath a colorful cloth canopy, similar to the Jewish huppah, supported by the bridesmaids and groomsmen. Sadly, as in so many countries, the most colorful aspects of the traditional Finnish wedding have not survived up to the present day. In western Finland, however, they do put on theatrical performances in the open which show a typical old-fashioned wedding, including the ceremony. Occasionally, for the ceremony itself, the actors stand aside and a young couple take their place, actually to be married in a consecrated glade in the forest with all the old majesty and magic, undeterred by the scores of strangers who make up the audience.

As in all peasant communities, life in rural Germany revolved around the success of the staple crop, which was commonly personified in Germany under the name of Corn-mother. In springtime when the wind ripples the standing corn, the peasants would say, "Here comes the Corn-mother," or "the Corn-mother is running through the fields." This belief is also shown when the corn is cut and the last small section is left standing to be cut by a specially selected young woman known as the Oats-bride or the Wheat-bride. When she has completed her task all other harvesters rejoice and crown her with a wreath made up of ears of corn. It is believed that the girl so chosen will be a real bride within the year.

Whether mock or real, German peasant weddings were always the occasion for much eating, drinking and general jollification. The engagement would usually take place the day before the first banns were read in Church and was a formal ceremony before witnesses and was marked by an exchange of gifts. The girl would present her fiancé with his wedding shirt and an embroidered handkerchief while he would present her with a pair of beautifully decorated slippers—a symbol of the wife's future subjection to her husband. Should this not turn out to be the case, then the henpecked husband would be said to be under his wife's slipper. After the banns, only a few weeks would pass before the actual wedding ceremony took place. During this time the young couple would choose one of their male friends and ask him to be their official wedding inviter. If he accepted, he would dress himself in his best clothes and decorate himself with flowers and ribbons, completing his toilet by tying a wreath of flowers to his walking-stick. With this he would knock resoundingly upon the doors of those fortunate enough to be receiving an invitation. Naturally he would be warmly welcomed and pressed to stay for a drink, or two. It has been known for the wedding messenger to fall by the wayside and never deliver his last few invitations but no one minded as everyone knew who had been invited anyway.

On the day of the wedding the bride would usually wear a special dress that had been handed down in her family for generations. She would also wear an elaborate crown made of wire, tinsel, artificial pearls and flowers, lots of ribbon and hair pins. It was a matter of pride to make this crown look as impressive as possible and the bride would get up especially early to have it constructed on her. At both the bride and groom's homes guests would be gathered to sample the morning soup and the first drinks of the day. Then the groom would set off to collect the bride. In some regions he would find her surrounded by her bridesmaids all dressed identically, in others he would find her in the guise of a burly,

A fanciful depiction of a pre-Christian German wedding. Pagan elements have survived in many festivals and rituals, not least the modern wedding ceremony. But in Nazi Germany deliberate—and ultimately unsuccessful—attempts were made to "paganize" weddings.

bearded man dressed in bride's finery. In some, he would not find her at all until he had conducted a rigorous search, for she would have been securely hidden by her friends. These customs seem to stem equally from a desire to show that the bride was unwilling to leave her family and maiden state and from a hope that by hiding or disguising the real bride, the evil spirits would not be able to sour her married life. Once the bride had been found, the young couple would go by cart to the church, probably being stopped on the way by young men barricading the road and demanding payment of a toll; this the groom would have had the foresight to bring with him.

At the church, the bride and groom would once again defeat the wicked spirits by walking up the aisle as close together as possible. In this way the spirits would be unable to come between them. As they knelt before the priest the groom would take care to kneel on the hem of the bride's dress to ensure that she was obedient to him in the years to come, but she could redress the balance by standing on his foot as they rose to stand before the priest again. After the ceremony, the newly married couple would lead the procession of guests to their new home in the wedding cart. On arrival a beer stein would be hurled over the roof, to keep the groom from drinking too much, while he was carrying the bride over the threshold. Once inside, they would share a morsel of bread together which would ensure that they would always have enough to eat in the future, then the bride would be pushed into the kitchen by her new husband where she would symbolically assume the mantle of housewife by salting the soup. The guests would then be invited inside after handing over a small gift to persuade the husband to open the door of his "castle"; the more honored members of the community would be invited in without such payment and would make up the top table at the forthcoming wedding feast. The wedding feasts of old were monumental meals of pork, goose, mutton, beef, dumplings, cabbage, potatoes, fish and bread: all this, of course, washed down with wine, beer and brandtwein in copious quantities. After the first course had been taken, the man chosen as official inviter would assume the role of toastmaster and lift his glass to the bride and groom, downing the contents in one and hurling his glass over his shoulder in such a way as to ensure that it smashed and brought the union good luck. This done, he called out the names of the guests one by one and they came forward and presented their gifts, being rewarded by the bridegroom with a drink from a jug. After this the musicians would begin to tune up for the dancing, the bride would rise, give an exclamation of pain and take off her shoe. There to her "surprise" she would discover a coin, which she would present to the musicians. She then led the dancing with her new husband. Once the first course was shaken down, the guests would return to the table but before the succeeding courses were served the cook would appear with her hand bound in a roll of cloth and demand money for medicine. This matter being settled, the serious eating and drinking began.

When the clock struck midnight the bride would have her bridal crown removed and be blindfolded. The bridesmaids would dance round her in a circle and a game of blind man's bluff would go on until one of the bridesmaids was caught. This girl, it was thought, would be the next to marry. Then the married women would chase the bride and force upon her head the bonnet that symbolized her married state: after this, three candles would be placed upon the floor and the bride would dance around them with each of the bridegroom's male relatives in turn. If the candles remained alight, all was well for the future. Eventually the guests would accompany the young couple to their marriage bed, in which someone would have placed pieces of bread and coal to appease yet again those evil spirits and then, to the accompaniment of a good deal of broad and suggestive humor, the bride and groom would finally be left alone.

Although there are obviously many survivals from the pagan era in these old customs, the actual wedding ceremony was very much a matter for the church. Religious feeling has always been strong in Germany. During the Nazi era, Himmler tried to combat it within the S.S. by deliberately introducing a policy of neo-paganism and by calling upon its members to repudiate the church. Himmler tried to make the S.S. an "Order of Germanic clans" and in 1936 laid down rules to ensure that its members understood it was their duty to marry and raise a family. In order to do so they had to be medically examined, show proof of their pure Aryan origin and submit photographs of themselves in bathing costumes. If they were accepted, the bride and groom were entered in the S.S. clan book and were then allowed to marry. The ceremony had to be a civil one at which only the immediate relatives were present. This was followed by a ceremony conducted by the local S.S. commander and based upon what were believed to be the old pagan rituals of exchanging iron rings and eating bread and salt before witnesses. In order to secure promotion to the senior ranks of the S.S. a member had to demonstrate that he had severed all links with his church. Despite this a very high proportion of members of the S.S. continued to practice their religion, and in 1937 307 S.S. men were expelled from the organization because they had married in the church. More and more of them continued to do so and in 1940 Himmler gave in to the inevitable and ordered that all men who had been so expelled could be readmitted to the S.S. provided they were satisfactory in all other respects. In view of the S.S. leadership, this determination to follow the traditional form of wedding ceremony has to be credited to the wives and mothers of S.S. members. In the face of such implacable opposition even the ruthless S.S. gave way.

In the free Germany of today the wedding is still generally both a family and a religious occasion. Engagements are taken seriously and regarded as binding. Both young people wear a plain gold ring during this period on the fourth fingers of their left hands. In south Germany the engagement is considered of such a binding nature that the boy and girl are known from the day of their engagement as "bridegroom" and "bride." According to German law, the wedding ceremony has to be carried out by an appointed official, who must not be a priest, at the local registry office. This somewhat impersonal ceremony is, however, often followed by a church ceremony on the following day. On the evening of the first day a party is still often held in the old tradition of *polterabend* when neighbors gather together to drink, dance and make as much noise as possible, smashing crockery and glass, banging saucepans and cracking whips all in the hope of driving away those ever-hovering evil spirits who might be jealous of the newly married couple's happiness. A good deal of drinking and merrymaking accompanies this assault on the spirits and it tends to go on until the early hours of the morning.

Hangovers notwithstanding, the young couple and their guests are at the church next morning. The bride today usually wears white while the groom will wear his best, dark business suit or a tuxedo. They enter the church together and are preceded by young children scattering flowers. At the appropriate moment during the ceremony they move the engagement rings they have been wearing from their left hands to their right. In later life, after one of the two has died, the surviving partner will wear the other's wedding ring on top of his or her own.

When the young couple leave the church after the wedding service they are likely to find their way barred by young children of the neighborhood, who will hold a rope or string across their path until the groom buys their way to freedom with a ransom of sweets and small coins, which one of his party will wisely have had ready. Nothing now stands in the way of the wedding reception which is usually held either at the home of the bride's parents or at a restaurant. During the reception the usual sentimental speeches are made and the customary toasts drunk and although the variety of food consumed is perhaps not as great as in the preceding centuries a good time is had by all and the party often lasts until late at night. In the country districts of Germany some of the old customs still survive and the wedding celebrations tend to include a much wider variety of guests taken from the whole of the immediate rural community.

But in most European countries today common religions and mass communication have led to the majority of wedding ceremonies being similar in form. To study national customs and traditions we have to go back in time.

For example, the Dutch in the seventeenth century were different from most of their European neighbors in that they practiced a high degree of married fidelity whilst speaking of sexual pleasures with a remarkable freedom and directness of expression. This probably arose partly out of national character and partly out of the fact that, contrary to European custom, marriages were not often arranged but arose out of personal preference on both sides. Various occasions were used for the

94

boys to meet suitable girls, and even church services had their place. Here the neighborhood boys could eye the girls at their leisure and chose the ones they would ask to go skating in the winter or to come on picnics in the sand-dunes in the summer. On May Day there would be celebrations around the bonfire and in some areas the boys would climb on to the roof of the girl of their choice and fix a green bough to the chimney.

Marriage was thought to be the best state for a woman and mothers began preparing their daughter's trousseau almost from the cradle. They also trained their daughters in their household duties, and extended this training to the art of acceptable flirtation so that they could attract a man and make a good match. When a girl had caught the eye of a young man, he showed that his intentions were serious by fixing a flowery wreath to her door. It was not thought proper for the girl to accept his suit at once and so the wreath would be unfixed and left lying at the threshold. The determined lover would fix a fresh wreath daily until the girl decided to let it remain. As a further sign of her acceptance of the courtship, she would place a small basket of sweetmeats in her window.

The lover could then make his first formal visit to her home. He would greet her parents and be welcomed. They would then tactfully retire and leave the young couple seated side by side for a long, silent communing that might last several hours. After this the boy was accepted as an official suitor and would visit the girl each night, climbing in through the window and getting into her bed where he lay between the sheet and eiderdown whilst the girl lay decorously between the sheets. As an added precaution against improper behavior, the girl would have an empty metal saucepan and some fire-irons within easy reach. Should the young man wax overamorous she could clatter these and summon her parents, at least that was the idea. In fact many a Dutch bride got married with her baby concealed beneath her cloak, suggesting that either Dutch parents were hard of hearing or the fire-irons were too heavy to lift.

After a period of getting to know each other, the young couple would become formally engaged, exchanging rings in the presence of both their families and kissing each other publicly for the first time. In some parts of Holland the engagement ceremony had rather more dramatic overtones. The young couple would cut their fingers and swallow each other's blood or sign a pact in their blood guaranteeing to be faithful to each other in the years to come. Engagements were generally short and the period prior to the wedding was a busy one. The engaged couple would choose their particular friends to be their official "playfellows" and they would all set about preparing for the wedding. The best room in the house would be decorated as lavishly as possible. First, all the mirrors in the house would be collected and hung on the walls. These were then wreathed with greenery and flowers and a carpet would be hung from the wall and ceiling to form a backdrop and a canopy to the two chairs upon which the bride and groom would sit. Whilst the young people got on with decorating, the parents saw to it that the engagement was registered with the municipal officials and that the banns were called three times in the church where the actual ceremony would take place. For this the church was decorated in the same way as the house had been. When the groom had answered "Yes," he placed the engagement ring he had been wearing onto the second finger of the bride's right hand above the engagement ring she was already wearing; sometimes these rings were worn on the thumb. After the ceremony the bride and groom would lead a procession of their pages and bridesmaids, families and friends back through the streets with children strewing flowers in front of them and over them.

Marriages in France in the twelfth century, among the landed classes, were arranged to increase the wealth and power of the two sets of parents, or of the groom if he was already an adult. The women were treated as mere attachments to tracts of land and coffers of gold, with little consideration given to their feelings whatsoever. Wives of princes

These exquisitely carved clogs commemorate a Dutch wedding in the late nineteenth century.

and noblemen could be imprisoned immediately after the day of the wedding or sent into virtual exile in the country or to a convent.

The feudal heiress was totally at the mercy of her father and had to do exactly as she was told. She was seen as an integral part of his estate and was no more than a visible sign of the transfer of assets between her father and the man to whom she was married. Sometimes she might even be handed out as a reward to a faithful retainer who had performed some service for her father.

Although the Catholic Church was totally opposed in theory to dissolving marriages, in fact it complied with the wishes of the feudal lords of the time and many women were divorced and married three or four times to fit in with the plans of their overlord. The Church also stood out strongly against marriages between close relatives; originally it opposed marriages between cousins, even to seventh cousins, but here again it had to fall in with local seigneurs and families intermarried in a complex web of relationships in order to strengthen their control over their estates.

The Catholic Church was determined to bring about obedience to its rulings and in the thirteenth century it had established a good deal more authority over the aristocracy in France and was almost completely in command in so far as the prosperous trading classes were concerned. With the merchants, as with their overlords, arranged marriages were the rule and the joining of business and fortunes was the thing uppermost in the minds of the parents. The Church, however, did not favor all this emphasis on finance and did all it could to discourage it. Although it could not stop two sets of parents arranging a marriage, the Church did stress the importance of the boy and girl who were to be married consenting to the match. It was also laid down that a bride must be twelve and the bridegroom fourteen before the wedding could take place and that they must not be closely related.

Once a wedding had been agreed upon between two merchant families, a marriage contract would be drawn up specifying the dowry that the bride was going to bring with her and also laying down what of her future husband's property would pass to her should he die before her. That done and witnessed by a notary, the couple would be officially betrothed. This was a religious ceremony that took place before a priest. The boy and the girl would signify their intention to marry should the Church find no barrier to their union and they would exchange rings. Then the banns would be published on three successive Sundays and the wedding day would be fixed. On that day the bride would be dressed by her mother in her best clothes: linen chemise, silk dress, velvet surcoat and a cloak finely edged with gold thread. On her head she would wear a small veil held in place by a band of gold. The groom would also dress in his finest clothes and together they would ride to church with a group of musicians going on in front while relatives and friends followed behind in procession. On arriving at the church door they would all dismount and be received by the priest. He asked them whether they were legally fit to be married and also about their individual willingness to go through with the ceremony. All being well, the young couple clasped hands and repeated their vows. The priest then addressed them on the blessed state of matrimony, its duties and their responsibilities. After this, he would bless the ring and the groom would place it in turn on each of the three fingers of the bride's left hand, saying "In the name of the Father, and of the Son, and of the Holy Ghost." Lastly he would place it on the third finger, saying "With this ring I thee wed."

For the middle and upper classes there was little real change until 1789. The revolutions in Russia and in China aimed, in part, to change the social pattern surrounding weddings—and for a time did so; the change does not look like it will last for very long, however. The French Revolution did have a much longer lasting effect upon marriage patterns. By attempting to introduce freedom, logic and lack of religious influence all at once, the authorities muddled the people and reduced their respect for the institution of marriage. Divorce was easily come by and many marriages lasted a very brief time indeed. This state of affairs outlasted both the Directory and Napoleon for many years, indeed up until the early part of the twentieth century. Like most revolutionary regimes one of the first actions of the French was to try and reduce the influence of established religion. Then the fanatic Hébert founded a religion worshipping the goddess "Reason," and after his death on the guillotine Robespierre instituted an alternative "Cult of the Supreme Being." During the new ceremony, local magistrates read appropriate passages from the new laws to the happy couple and then made an address reminding them of their duty to each other and to the State. Wedding ceremonies were usually held between set hours and tended to follow closely upon each other's heels. They proved to be a popular form of public entertainment and any couple who looked anything out of the ordinary was greeted with cheers, jeers and songs. An official of the Directory who attended the wedding between a black man and a white woman was much shocked at the bad behavior of the self-invited guests, and wrote to the minister of the interior to report on the event.

Courtly love or dynastic alliance? The marriage of Philippe d'Artois, Comte d'Eu, and Marie, daughter of the Duc de Berry, early fifteenth century.

Citizen Minister,

I denounce the public to you, yesterday it behaved with the utmost lack of decorum.

During the marriage ceremony at the Temple de la Paix in the Xth arrondissement, there was such a noise and general commotion that the reading of the laws and the address to the congregation could not be heard. The orchestra added to the disorder by playing tunes deliberately angled to create laughter. When the couple appeared they began to play an aria from *Azema*, "Ivory with ebony makes pretty jewels," the crowd joined in with much laughter.

If this kind of mockery is not stopped, Citizen Minister, it could reduce the number of marriages. Certainly, several young women stated, in my hearing, that they would rather remain spinsters all their lives than provide amusement for the public and be mocked in public.

The Emperor Napoleon was anxious for religious respectability, for both spiritual and political reasons, and encouraged the Catholic Church to emerge from the shadows. Gradually religious wedding ceremonies began to become the accepted form again. Indeed, Napoleon married Josephine twice: at a civil ceremony in 1796, and some years later at a church ceremony. At first weddings took place very early in the morning to avoid drawing attention to themselves, and the civil ceremony at the town hall followed. After the Concordat, the agreement signed between the Pope and the Emperor in 1802, the civil ceremony generally took place first and the church service later in the day; for many fashionable weddings the church ceremony was held at night. The daughter of the minister of foreign affairs got married at the ultra-fashionable hour of midnight. Her cousin wrote a letter describing the occasion:

On Wednesday I got a most friendly letter from my aunt inviting us to attend the wedding. This was to take place at night . . . we arrived at the town hall at eight-thirty and the Mayor made a curious speech, among other oddities he asked the bride to assume "paternal" feelings and added that he was sure that the union would be a happy one because it arose as a consequence of their parents' desires and of a long established affection. (They have known each other for ten days!) Following upon the civil ceremony

Clerks, soldiers and the flame of "Reason" epitomize this wedding during the French Revolution.

we left to take supper and then moved on to the church, which was ablaze with light. There was a large congregation, nine carriage loads of guests, and the rector gave a long address. I am sure that even if it had been longer no one would have tired of listening to it. I was truly edified to see how the people behaved in church. The fathers and grandmothers of the bride and groom knelt throughout the address and through the Mass.

No laughter or mockery here—religion and respect had made a comeback—but the bride and groom had only known each other for ten days. This reflected a major change in social behavior but one that is not unusual in time of war. Gallant soldiers return from the battle zone eager to ensure the continuance of their line. Impressionable young women full of patriotism and pity succumb to rapid courtship. The courtship is brief, the honeymoon even briefer for the husband has to return to the front. If he returns and settles down with his bride, possibly now a mother, they will soon know whether or not love at first sight is a sound basis for marriage. All too often it was not and these rapid marriages would be followed by a divorce almost as swift.

In his diary Stendhal noted that: "The Abbé Hélie, who has heard the confessions of many and thus has been able to study mankind at close quarters, tells me that there are only twenty-five good marriages out of a hundred, that is unions between people who truly love one another. A further fifty couples will at least get on well with one another, although the husband will often be cuckolded." Perhaps this somewhat cynical view accounted for the fact that marriage as an institution took a sharp knock at this point in French history. In the department of the Seine the married only outnumbered the unmarried by twenty percent, while of the total number of births in Paris, thirty-three percent were registered as illegitimate.

Gradually the stability of French family life returned and although many changes can be seen in the ruling classes in France during the period between the First and Second World Wars, the solid rural middle class and peasantry continued to display an indifference to changing fashions and to lead lives notable for hard work and thriftiness. Saving, in France, was a national habit. The incentive was twofold: first, the anxiety to make provision for old age; second, the necessity for putting by a dowry for each daughter who was not prepared to give up the idea of marriage and become a member of a religious order. A contemporary English writer on the social life of the Third Republic saw the situation as follows. "The dowry must be ready if suitable husbands are to be attracted. Love matches have been a little more frequent in recent years, but the rule is still for marriages to be arranged by parents upon a financial basis. It is hard for English people to believe that this can give such good results as their own system of unfettered choice, but it appears to be followed by quite as many successful unions as can be counted in England. I say 'successful' rather than happy, because I do not think that, while on the whole French husbands and wives get along comfortably together, and are more often partners in the fullest sense than are English married couples, yet they do not as often know the happiness of married life."

France, the land of love, turns out to be the land of practicality in fact. Italy in the time of Casanova had the reputation of being a land of liberty. Facts once again dispel the myth. Chastity and fidelity have always been demanded of Italian women both now and in the past.

In the Italian upper classes during the eighteenth century, marriages were arranged between the families with little consultation of the parties directly involved. No considerations of romance were normally allowed to influence such matters but in Venice some lip service was paid to the idea. Once a marriage had been arranged the young man was supposed to demonstrate his instant dedication to his bride-to-be by walking up and down outside her window at the fashionable hour. His fiancée would be sitting there awaiting him and would smilingly acknowledge his devotion. The actual wedding normally took place at home before an assembly of all the most important relations dressed as magnificently as possible. The bride would wear a dress of silver brocade, her bosom covered with fine lace and jewels. Her entrance to the reception room where the ceremony was to take place was most theatrical. She would stop just within the doorway and give her hand to a master of ceremonies dressed in black and wearing a damask cloak. He would lead her to a velvet cushion upon which she would kneel to receive the blessings of her parents and her closest relations. She would then rise and be led by the master of ceremonies to the center of the room where her husband-to-be awaited her. Her hand would be placed in his and the union would then be blessed by the priest. The couple then kissed and the bride led the dancing by performing a solitary minuet. As the demands of fashion increased, this latter part of the ceremony was postponed to allow the ladies to change their dresses. They attended the ceremony in dresses of black silk trimmed with lace which they discarded for gaily colored silks for the ball. The bride would often change also, into another white dress, and would exchange the pearls that were traditionally worn for the ceremony for jewels of a more spectacular kind.

Naturally such expensive celebrations were not the case in peasant weddings, but the customs practiced, particularly in Sicily, were elaborate and had direct links with the ancient past. In the poorest society, as in the wealthiest, the bride and groom had little say in whom they were to marry. A mother would choose a bride for her son from among the girls of the village and would signal her choice by dropping a brush at the door of the selected girl at sun-rise. The girl would pick it up and would make sure that she was sitting in her best clothes at mid-day when her future mother-in-law would arrive to re-braid her hair with a ribbon in a special way that signified a betrothal.

On the day of the wedding, the groom's family and friends would go in procession, singing traditional wedding songs to fetch the bride. On the arrival at the bride's cottage, the groom's father would go in alone and compliment her on the fine attire upon which she and her female relatives would have been working over the years. He would then lead her to the door where the groom awaited her. As they exchanged greetings, they would be showered with wheat, bread and salt as an earnest of the fecund years ahead. The bride's mother would then attach a thin biscuit to the groom's buttonhole with ribbons; this represented the food with which he would supply his family in the time to come. The party would then walk to the church where the priest would cense them and bless them before putting a gold ring on the groom's index finger and a silver one on the bride's. These rings would then be exchanged three times and then the couple would be crowned with wreaths of bay leaves, olive branches and rosemary, the wreaths in turn being exchanged three times. The priest would place a light veil of white over both their heads, covering the wreaths and uniting them. The young couple would then take a lighted candle in one hand each and link their little fingers.

A cloth-covered table would be set up in the church upon which would stand bread and wine. The priest would break the bread and dip it into the wine, giving the young couple three small pieces each before making them take three sips of wine apiece from the same glass. This glass he would then break, supposedly to demonstrate the extreme fragility of human happiness. Following this brief note of gloom, the priest, the happy couple and the witnesses would form a circle and dance three times around the table. After this, they and the other guests would leave the church in procession for the wedding reception at which there would be large empty dishes set aside to receive the guests' wedding presents. It is interesting to note the strong similarity of this Roman Catholic ceremony to that of the peasant community Greek Orthodox ceremony. In continental Europe, as in the rest of the world, there is an amazing similarity between wedding customs, a similarity that cannot be accounted for by religious practice or intercommunication. It would seem to spring from common human needs rooted in the basic relationship between mankind and his environment.

RIGHT *In most Arab societies the bride is shown unveiled only to the female guests and members of the family. In this photograph of the bride she cannot be seen at all!* **INSET** *But among the Berbers the bride's full beauty can be remarked upon by all.*

ABOVE *A colorfully clad couple from Lagartera, Spain, share a joke as they embark on a shared life.*

LEFT *The national flag of Israel forms the huppah at a kibbutz wedding. The pitchforks and rifles supporting the huppah symbolize the duality of kibbutz life.*

TURKEY TO TIMBUCTOO:
THE MIDDLE EAST AND AFRICA

"Blest is the bride on whom the sun doth shine" ROBERT HERRICK

TURKEY'S GREATEST DAYS were undoubtedly during the period of the Ottoman Empire which lasted from the end of the thirteenth century until the end of the First World War. Naturally its power as an empire rose and declined, and it was at its most powerful at the time when Elizabeth I was on the throne of England, when its rule extended all through the present-day territories of Iraq, Syria, Lebanon and Israel, Egypt, Libya, Tunisia and Algeria to the south of the Mediterranean, while to the north it held sway in Greece, Albania, Yugoslavia, Bulgaria, Hungary and parts of southern Russia. Conquest completed, the Ottoman authorities brought their administrative abilities to bear upon these territories and established the rule of law, within which a great variety of religious and social practices was permitted. Within Turkey itself society was remarkably stable and many customs remained virtually unchanged for the whole six hundred years or so of the empire. This was certainly the case of the wedding arrangements for the Muslim majority of the population.

A boy was adjudged by his father to be ready for marriage when he reached the age of puberty, around thirteen or fourteen. His mother would then take over the handling of the whole affair, for it was her immediate duty to secure a suitable bride for her son. She would immediately set about seeking out a likely girl through information given to her by members of her family and friends. Note would be taken of the homes of those girls that sounded suitable and one by one they would be called upon by the mother and a retinue of advisers. On arriving at a selected house, they would announce the reason for the visit to the senior lady of the household, who would invite them in warmly and entertain them while the potential bride was dressed in her best clothes by her attendants. When she was ready, she would shyly enter the presence of the visitors and serve them coffee while they examined her closely to see if she was suitable. This ordeal was ended when the visiting mother handed the young girl back her coffee cup; she then had to withdraw. A really thorough mother would arrange for a prospective wife to appear at an agreed time at the ladies' baths when she could be examined in the greatest detail. These examinations were made quite obviously, and audibly, but the blushing maiden had to pretend to be totally unaware of what was going on.

The boy's mother would formally ask the mother of the most suitable girl for her hand in marriage on behalf of her son and would give details of his family, job and prospects. The whole affair would then be handed over to the two fathers, who would begin to investigate the realities of the social and financial position of the family to which each might be linked. If these inquiries proved satisfactory to both sides, matters proceeded. If not, the affair was dealt with delicately by the dissatisfied party, saying that the omens were unfavorable. This was quite acceptable, as dreams during this preliminary period had much importance attached to them, and were eagerly interpreted as being good or bad omens. A succession of ill-starred dreams would be accepted by either party as a reason to break off the tentative engagement.

The idea of asking the girl whether she wanted to marry the boy chosen for her was never considered, and almost as little consideration was given to the wishes of the boy. They would never have met and the groom would neither see nor speak to his bride until the wedding was over. As in so many other societies, family considerations came first and alliances were sometimes cemented by two families betrothing their respective children in infancy. Where neither power nor great wealth was in question, the families concerned linked themselves through similarities in trade or profession. Despite the lack of choice, girls looked forward to their wedding and prepared for it from early childhood, sewing and preparing clothes and household linen for their dowries. At the age of twelve or so they put on the veil and looked upon themselves as marriageable women.

There was no religious wedding ceremony; marriage was regarded as a legal contract undertaken between two families. After the betrothal and the dowry agreement, an actual contract was drawn up and copies were held by both families. The exchange of contracts was carried out, before two witnesses of the Muslim faith, and would be made widely known in the locality where each family lived. Thus would the marriage be declared legal and binding, and a day would be selected as the most auspicious for the wedding feast: if possible, a Friday; if not, then a Monday would be chosen.

On the Wednesday night the groom's friends were entertained by his parents at a lively party with gypsy dancers and music while the bride and her female friends and relatives followed an old-established custom and stained the bride's hands and feet with scarlet henna. Into her hand would be pressed a gold coin, also liberally bedaubed with henna, and then both her hands and her feet would be bandaged to ensure that the henna stayed on all night. The next day the bride received a gift of clothes from the groom. She immediately dressed in them and was led before her family, where she formally kissed her father's hand. He then tied a scarf around her waist, drew out his sword and held it close to the floor with the command: "Jump over this sword and bring forth children who will use it as well as did your ancestors." He would recite solemn prayers and the family would weep at the thought of the forthcoming parting and the end of the bride's childhood.

On Friday, the auspicious day having come at last, the young bride went in procession to the house of the groom's parents and was seated in a room especially decorated with greenery and silk hangings. Around her was displayed her dowry, the best items being well to the fore, and the whole room was hung with garlands of artificial flowers lovingly prepared by her friends. There she sat as a stream of visitors came to inspect her and her worldly goods. The groom meanwhile had gone to the mosque with his companions, and they returned in procession, to loud shouts of "the groom is coming." At the door of the bridal chamber he would be met by the chief attendant upon the bride and led up to her, whereupon she would shyly kiss his hand and remove her veil in his presence for the first time. To mark this great moment, the groom would embrace the bride and give her a piece of jewelry as an "unveiling" gift. The young couple would then immediately part, the groom to join the men and the bride the women in their separate quarters where the festivities would continue for the rest of the day.

After all the celebrations were over, the bride would move to her new husband's family's house and become subject to her mother-in-law's control and guidance. There she would concentrate upon pleasing her husband and producing as many male children as possible.

The proclamation of the Republic of Turkey in 1923 was followed by a succession of legislation aimed at modernizing the country as quickly as possible. The Civil Code, which affected marriage, was introduced in 1926 and was based almost entirely upon the similar code then extant in Switzerland. This code brought about the emancipation of women and abolished and prohibited polygamy. It also introduced civil marriage before a registrar and increased the number of legal impediments to divorce. The age when a person came of age was set at eighteen but a court could declare a person an adult at fifteen. As a result the courts were swamped with requests to do just that from engaged couples; tens of thousands of such actions were brought. Consequently, in 1938, the age for marriage was set at seventeen for men and fifteen for women. The new marriage laws were very unpopular, and the peasants in particular resented them. They could not understand the need for appearing before a registrar, and the inevitable filling-in of forms that accompanies any new bureaucratic regulation was beyond their capabilities. They also strongly resisted the medical examination of the bride which was laid down under the new code. This outraged their sense of decency.

They showed their distaste for the new laws by largely ignoring them and by getting married as they always had, even though this meant that their children were legally branded as illegitimate. Hundreds of thousands of children were affected so that special provisions were made several times between 1933 and 1965 to allow them to be registered as legitimate. Once again the human desire to follow the old wedding customs has overcome the wishes of officialdom.

Before the people of Iran were converted to the Islamic faith they were adherents of the Zoroastrian religious system. Its principles are contained in the *Zend-Avesta* and include a belief in the afterlife and in the continuous conflict between Ormuzd, the god of Light and Good, and Ahriman, the god of Darkness and Evil. They believe that the good will ultimately prevail. The followers of this religion were subject to Muslim persecution in the seventh and eighth centuries and some, the Parsees, fled to India, where they still practice their beliefs.

The Zoroastrians believe that marriage is divinely favored, and that the second happiest place in existence is that where a righteous man sets up his household. Acting upon this belief, they gain religious credit in helping others to wed and rich Parsees will leave money to a trust set up to provide dowries for poor brides. The Zoroastrian wedding ceremony is preceded by a variety of other rites. When the match is arranged, usually at the wish of the two young people, a favorable day is decided by the astrologers for the betrothal ceremony. On this day the women of the groom's family visit the house of the bride and make her a present of silver coins, while the groom receives a similar present from the women of the bride's family. In country areas the ceremony is attended by two priests—one for each family—who make a formal request to the parents of the bride and of the groom that they be given in marriage to each other. The engagement ceremony is followed by that of the lamp, when a lamp is lit early in the morning, and once again the women of the two families visit each other and exchange gifts. On this day the dresses and wedding rings are usually presented. The next important day is known as Adarni. On this occasion, the bride's father presents her dowry to the groom's family.

On the wedding day a procession, headed by the officiating priests and preceded by musicians, goes to the house of the bride. The men seat themselves in the compound whilst the women sit separately in the house. When the groom arrives at the door of the compound he is greeted by his future mother-in-law, who marks his forehead with a red pigment, on to which some rice is pressed, while more is thrown over his head. He then passes between the door posts which have been smeared with turmeric, the yellow color of which symbolizes the life-giving qualities of the sun. He crosses the threshold right foot first and without touching it. Then the groom sits in the compound surrounded by male friends and relatives. He wears a white ceremonial robe, with a garland of flowers around his neck and a shawl held in his hand. An egg, a coconut and a little tray of water are now passed three times round the groom's head and are then thrown away.

Within the house chairs are set out facing each other for the bride and groom. Beside the chairs are little tables carrying dishes of rice and lighted candles, the table beside the bride's chair also carrying jugs of butter and sugar syrup symbolizing the smooth, sweet nature of her future conduct. Servants stand before the chairs burning frankincense and the witnesses to the ceremony are also assembled. When the groom and bride enter they are at first seated opposite each other, curtained from each other's view by a piece of cloth. The senior priest then joins their right hands and recites holy texts as he encircles both chairs with a piece of cloth whose ends he ties together. To the accompaniment of further texts, the right hands of the young couple are then bound together by twine. This passes seven times around their hands, then seven times around them both and, finally, seven times around the knot that is tying together the encircling cloth. More frankincense is burned and the dividing curtain is dropped—a signal for the bride and groom to throw over each other the grains of rice which they have been holding in their left hands. They then move their chairs so that they are sitting side by side, the bride on the left.

The ritualistic part of the ceremony is now over and the religious

A splendid portrayal of a splendid wedding in seventeenth-century Persia. As always, food, drink, music and dancing play their part.

service begins. Two priests stand in front of the couple and the elder blesses them, calling upon Ahura Mazda to grant them "progeny of sons and grandsons, abundant means, strong friendship, bodily strength, long life and an existence of 150 years." The priest then asks the witness representing the groom's family whether he consents to the wedding. He then puts the same question to the witness on the bride's side. These questions are repeated three times. Next the priest reads admonitions from the holy texts calling upon the married pair to lead an exemplary life together. Finally, blessings are called upon the heads of the young couple and Ahura Mazda is asked to grant them the moral and social virtues that characterize the angels, *yazatas*, who give their names to the thirty days of the month.

In some country districts the robes of the bride and groom are tied together by their nearest friends and relatives and they go, thus united, to the bridegroom's house. There the feet of both are ritually washed or rather, since the introduction of western style footwear, the tips of their shoes are washed. This completed, the newly married couple take their first food together consisting of curd and rice eaten from the same dish and served to each other.

After this, the guests are invited to sit down to the wedding feast, which is enlivened by song and which must include fish dishes, thought to be a good omen, and sweets.

Naturally the Zoroastrian wedding ceremony varies from district to district but in every area it must, to be accepted, be celebrated in front of at least five specially invited people. Additionally, the contracting parties must be asked by the officiating priest whether they consent to be joined in wedlock, their hands must be joined by the priest and a symbolic knot must play a significant part in the ceremony. Finally, the actual wedding ceremony must be followed by a blessing from the priest accompanied by a sprinkling with rice.

In Arab countries great weight is given to the sexual purity of the female. Undervalued in every other way, the woman in Arab Islamic society has always been overvalued in this respect. To protect her purity she was supposed to don the veil at the age of ten or eleven and remain from then until marriage in the harem with the older women. The girl had no choice in whom she might marry, while the young man could only indicate a choice to his parents. He had no money of his own to pay the bride price and relied upon his parents to do so. Once it was decided that a young man should marry, the women of his household would visit all the families in the neighborhood who had daughters

124

This Bedouin girl from Saudi Arabia is adorned with coins presented by her father. They form part of her dowry, but her husband has no claim to it : it is hers in case of divorce.

of a marriageable age and who were of the right social order. They would inspect the girls and decide upon one based upon their view of her beauty, character and wifely virtues. The men of the two families would then meet to discuss the drawing up of the marriage contract and the payment of the bride price. This price depended upon factors such as the girl's beauty, talents, character, the wealth of her family and their desire to keep her at home. The price tended to be high, sometimes equaling half the annual income of the groom's father. Amongst well-to-do families the bride price was usually spent on a trousseau of jewelry, furniture, clothes and so on and a sum at least its equal would be spent by the bride's family. These purchases were the property of the bride both during and after marriage by the terms of the marriage contract, which would be drawn up in the presence of witnesses and the local *imam*. This gave the girl some insurance against poverty if she were to be divorced and also acted as a disincentive to the husband's divorcing her, for usually only half of the agreed bride price was paid on the signing of the marriage contract. The other half was paid over only in the case of a divorce.

Over the past two decades certain improvements in the status of Arab women of the upper and middle classes have come about, but for the majority of Arabs, the poor and those living in rural areas, little real change has occurred and the customs they follow are those of their ancestors.

For the bride the transition from being a child in the harem to being a married woman is sudden and traumatic. Without any previous warning she will be called to the room of the senior woman of the household who will catch hold of her and say, "we are going to veil you and henna you, for you are to be the bride of Sayeed." Traditionally the young girl will weep and show every sign of reluctance as she is made to discard her white robe and be dressed in red with a black veil covering her head and face. From that moment on women attend her, their first task being to paint elaborate patterns on her hands and feet with henna. At the bridegroom's house the male members of his family and his men friends will have gathered in the courtyard to congratulate him. When they are all seated, the bridegroom will make a formal entrance and seat himself in front of them. A boy of the household will then put a round mat in front of him and some of the guests will throw onto it handfuls of coffee beans. They will be the honored guests at the first day of the wedding feast and the beans will be used to make their coffee. The boy attendant will then appear with a tray and make jokes with the guests about the groom's performance on the wedding night. He will then make a mock attack upon the groom and place the tray before the groom, whose father puts a gift of money into it. The groom strikes the tray with his dagger as a sign of his gratitude and this ceremony is repeated as guest after guest hands money to the boy, who calls out their names before putting the money in the tray. Next a bowl of liquid henna is passed around and the whole assembly rub henna over their hands. A period of quiet conversation follows but suddenly the groom will leap to his feet and make strenuous attempts to escape through the doorway, only to be prevented by his young friends. The occasion then ends with dancing and singing.

(The actual wedding ceremony is not attended by the bride.) It is in fact a ceremony of affirmation that the families of both bride and

A lavish—and presumably very noisy—bridal procession in Cairo. Eighteenth century.

groom agree that a marriage should take place and that the terms of the
marriage contract are agreed upon. The groom is present, and so are the
fathers, who place their hands together in the presence of the *imam*. He will
then say prayers and call down a blessing upon the union.

Afterwards there will be feasting for family, friends, retainers and
even casual visitors. Rice and mutton will be served on large trays and
tea will be served all day, with tiny cups of bitter coffee for the more
distinguished guests. The bride plays no part in this feasting as she is kept
locked in her room with her constant female companions. On the second
day her hair is dressed as a married woman's with two pieces left loose on
either side of her forehead. On the third day, the bride is dressed in her
red wedding garment and a combined wig and headdress is placed over
her hair. Her attendants load her down with gold necklaces, bangles and
other ornaments. If she comes from a wealthy family these may all be her
own but, if not, her family may well have borrowed them for the
occasion. She is then led to the bridegroom's bedroom accompanied by
her attendants, her female relatives and the servants and members of the
harem. She must say nothing and sit with eyes downcast, giving him no
assistance as he slowly undoes, one by one, all the items of jewelry.

The next morning the female servants wake the bridegroom early and send him out of the room. They wash the bride and settle her down to have an undisturbed sleep. Later in the day they will dress the bride in new finery and seat her in a room on two gold embroidered bridal cushions which will have texts pinned onto them. There she will be visited by the father of the groom and by her own father. She will say nothing and sit with her eyes modestly closed during the whole proceedings. A servant will first fill the room with the fumes of frankincense, another will bring in a tray of freshly roasted coffee beans for the two connoisseurs to sniff. They will then be taken away and served as coffee. Still no one has spoken. Silent to the end, the two men finally rise, place gifts of money in the bride's lap and leave.

Immediately after they have left, the bride's attendants cover her hair once more with the combined wig and headdress and lead her, preceded by female drummers, to a major reception area. Two servants carry the bridal cushions aloft and others burn more frankincense as the bride is seated in the center of the packed room. Her veil is then lifted as she sits there with her eyes downcast, and the guests gaze upon her. This exposure on the morning after her wedding night is her symbolic entrance into the world of married women. On the following day she will once again have her face exposed to the women outside in the courtyard and this is the final ceremony of the wedding. The feasting ends, the guests depart and the bride takes her place in her husband's house.

Although the Islamic faith followed the Arab trader into the interior of Africa, hundreds of tribes and peoples still continue to follow the customs of their ancestors unaffected by Islam, Christianity or the patterns of western society as expressed through the mass media. For many Africans the day of the wedding is still generally the day named on which the girl goes to her husband. At the appointed time conductors, who are often members of her family, lead her, usually after night has fallen, to her husband's house. This can be the signal for the firing of guns, dances or other performances but of anything resembling a western wedding there is usually not a trace.

The fact is that the essential rites, which make it a lawful union and not a runaway love match, have been performed years before, often when the bride was not old enough even to form an opinion of her husband to be. Among the Ibo people, on the Lower Niger, for example, a suitor will come with a load of wood and throw it down outside the door on the very day that a girl baby has arrived. If he is something of a gambler, he may carry out the ceremony even earlier. A week or two

Before an Ibo bride of good family marries she must go into a "fattening house." Then there will be a dance lasting several days. The bride here (center) is on day three of her dance.

later he carries to the father a pot of palm wine. If this is accepted, the suitor is officially recognized as the claimant to the young girl's hand. Before the wine has been accepted, however, the girl's father will have made detailed inquiries as to the suitor's character, the reputation of his family and so on. Once accepted, the suitor must bring yearly gifts to the father, mother and the girl. Over and above this, he may begin to pay the bride price which varies according to the economic circumstances of the tribe and to the status of the families concerned.

The suitor is also bound to give help to his future father-in-law when work has to be done in the cultivated plots of land around the village or to the living quarters of the girl's family. He may even be expected to persuade his young male friends to come and help if a major piece of forest clearing or harvesting has to be undertaken. The father of the girl gets all this valuable labor free except that he is expected to feed those helping him.

These early payments and practical assistance do no more than establish a claim upon the girl; after some years the Ibo will take the really important step which binds the girl to him and makes him the legal owner of any children she may bear, whoever the father may be, until the proper steps have been taken, by refund of the sums paid towards the bride price and so on, to depose him from his privileged position. Precisely how he will bind the girl to him depends upon tribal usage; it will, however, often take the form of a sacrifice to her ancestors, or it may consist of a formal meal taken together by the two families involved.

The marriage ceremony proper is performed after the bride has gone back to visit her parents some days later; she takes a fowl back to her husband as a sign that the union is ratified by the family.

Elsewhere, however, the rites are infinitely varied. Among the Baganda people, the suitor may approach the girl herself, or he may ask her brother who, in turn, will consult his uncle. If the suitor is accepted, he makes the rounds of his friends and relatives to collect from them the sum to be paid as bride price. Before she goes to her husband, the bride cuts grass—the native carpet—draws water and brings firewood as a symbolic last service to her parents; after shedding tears at leaving her father's house, she is conducted by a man, or men, to her new husband's house.

She goes after dark, but nevertheless wears a veil of bark down to her ankles. When she has gone halfway, her party is met by the suitor and his party and they then take charge of the bride. When the groom's house is reached, cowrie shells are given to the bride as she crosses the threshold and again when she sits down for the first time, and when she begins to eat. This ritual is carried out to symbolize her reluctant progress, by persuasion, towards accepting her new role.

Two or more forms of marriage may well exist in a single tribe. In West Africa the distinction has been between "bond" and "free" marriage. In the former the wife becomes the property of her husband, her children are his heirs, the husband buries his wife if she dies before him. If she becomes a widow, his heir inherits her as a wife. She is not a slave in status, but there is good reason to suppose that this kind of marriage originated in the setting free of a slave to become a wife. In the "free" marriage on the other hand, the woman may leave her husband at will; if she dies, her own family take the corpse and bury her, and the husband would have to pay damages if he infringed their rights and did so himself. The children of such a marriage belong to their mother's family and inherit from her relatives; if their father wishes them to become his heirs, he can only arrange it by purchasing them from the family of the mother.

Two other forms of married relationship also exist. If it happens that a man has no sons, then his property will pass to his brothers or other descendants. This he can avoid by retaining one of his daughters at home. She is not married through the ordinary way of wife purchase but takes a husband who comes to her in her father's house. Her children are reckoned as being the children of her father, not of her husband, and they are his heirs.

The other form of marriage is contracted when a woman has acquired wealth, possibly as a market trader, but has no children. Not willing for her hard-earned money to pass to her relatives, she "marries" a girl by purchase and selects a lover for her. Children of this union are not recognised as belonging to the girl or her lover but are the accepted heirs of the wealthy woman who purchased the girl in the first place.

A fairly definite ritual accompanies the going of a bride to her husband in the cases just described for the Ibo. It is possible for the westerner to identify with it in part at least. But the ceremonies surrounding marriage amongst the pygmy Mbuti who live in the forest around the Ituri River in central Africa bear very little resemblance to anything recorded in the west. The Mbuti, when not living on and in the villages of their non-pygmoid neighbors, roam the forest in bands. When a girl reaches puberty and menstruates for the first time she is known to be ready for marriage and her education for motherhood and wifely responsibility begins; it is time for the *elima* celebration. She gathers together a number of girls of her own age, and older, whom she likes and respects and invites them to join her *bamelima*, a group who live in a special hut and stay together for two to three months. Inside the hut they are taught how to be good wives and mothers by older women who impart all their knowledge by song. They also go off into the surrounding forest and commune with its "spirit."

The members of the *bamelima* also indulge in a good deal of sexual experimentation both amongst their own band and with the youths of other bands. This custom would seem to have a threefold aim: to extend the sexual knowledge and expertise of the girls, to widen their social experience by their meetings with members of other bands and to find a man who will make them a suitable husband. Sexual approaches are not indiscriminate but are controlled by a rigid code of practice. Every so often the girls of the *bamelima* will come out of their hut armed with broken branches and young trees and will pursue the young men of their choice beating them soundly. Any boy so beaten is honor bound to enter the girl's hut later that day where he will be beaten once again. If his bearing has impressed the young girl who chose him, she will let him make love to her but not let him hold her in his arms. In this way they believe that they will avoid conception and certainly no births have ever been traced back to this period. No doubt some of the herbal lore imparted in song by the older women includes knowledge of contraceptive medicine.

At first only young men from their own band visit the girls but later other bands visit and are visited. Not only future husbands are "invited": the young married men also participate, although they make love only to the older girls. Towards the end of this period of education and celebration, the mothers of the girls gather outside the hut towards nightfall with baskets of stones and other likely missiles. Now any youth can try to enter the hut and seek out the girl of his fancy but he has to run the gauntlet. If he is thought to be a desirable mate, then he has a fairly easy time of it. If the mothers think he is a ne'er-do-well, the brickbats will be heavy, sharp and accurate. Once inside he is beaten again and has to persuade the girl to let him make love to her. If his mission is successful, he then has to stay in the hut until the celebration is over, probably a week or so, and he and the girl of his choice will be considered to be betrothed. When the ceremony of *elima* is over, the boy will wait until an appropriate time and then formally approach the girl's parents for their approval. Having shown that he is a man prepared to suffer for what he wants, he now has to prove himself as a hunter and provider. Accordingly he will haunt the forest until he has been able to track down and kill a fine deer, which he will present to his future wife's parents. The girl will then build a hut and they will live together without further ado. When a girl becomes pregnant, the marriage will be considered to have taken place, the betrothal period being at an end. If pregnancy does not occur within the year, the couple will usually part and seek new partners but if they do wish to stay together then they will be considered to be married after having lived together for about another year.

The G'wi Bushmen of Botswana are married by agreement of their parents when the girl is very young and the boy but little older. They live in the same camp as the bride's parents and her father may well move into their hut also. The couple do not live together truly until after the girl has menstruated for the first time. When this happens she tells her mother immediately. Her mother, together with some of her friends, at once begins to build a wattle circle some little way away from the main camp. Here the girl has to sit absolutely still, legs straight out before her, for four days during which she must not speak or eat. However, the women do take her a little food and water occasionally and everyone pretends not to notice. As soon as the circle has been begun the groom leaves his hut and goes to sleep in the bachelors' hut, taking with him his hunting weapons which on no account must be touched by his wife lest, so he believes, he meet with a disaster when next out hunting.

After the four days' silent fast, the women bring the bride and groom together and shave their heads and wash their bodies all over using a sliced juicy bulb as a sponge. Great care is taken to ensure that the fibers used to wash the girl's body do not touch the boy. When they have been washed, the pair are then tattooed. They are cut with a razor on their hands, feet and back. The tattooing proceeds step by step so that the same parts of their bodies are dealt with at the same time. Their blood is taken and mixed together over the cuts to symbolize their union one with the other. While this painful process is going on, the older women of the clan sit around them and give them good advice about how to ensure a happy married life, and the importance of avoiding adultery. When the pattern of cuts has been completed, a mix of ashes and medicinal roots is rubbed in to ensure that the cuts will heal as raised blue scars.

The tattooing over, the girl will be led by one of the women into the center of the camp where the other women will be waiting, and where an edible plant will be pressed to her forehead. Her attendant will then turn her around and point to the distant circle of the horizon saying, "This is food. What you see is our world and yours. You will always find food here." After this, the bride is taken by the young women and made to run as fast as possible around the camp before being brought back into the hut where she has been living with her husband. The fast patter of the running feet is supposed to sound like the falling rain and, as they run, the young women shout with delight as though they were running through a refreshing shower. This sympathetic magic, it is believed, will cause the girl to attract rain which in turn will bring water and growth to the crops.

The groom now joins his bride in their hut and one of the older women will paint them both with identical designs carried out in red ocher and fat. The girl is then led out and handed over to her father. By this time all the inhabitants of the camp will have gathered around the father, as though by accident, ready for the next part of the ceremony. The girl is now supposed to be as blind as a newborn kitten and her father, who has raveled together a ball of grass, snaps it apart before her eyes and says, "Look at your people." He then introduces each member of the clan to his daughter as though they were complete strangers to her and gives a brief biographical sketch of each. To be amongst the first so described is an honor and is supposed to bring luck in hunting. The father uses the opportunity to make new friends and to pay off old scores. When the recital is over the people go back to their huts and bring out their most precious ornaments which they hang around the young couple who can wear them for a day or two before returning them to their owners.

Similar ceremonies will occur when the girl menstruates for the second and third time. Then the groom will cut two small sticks, decorate them and tie them at each end of a strip of hide. This he will give to the bride who will wear it around her neck as a sign that she is now a woman and a wife.

The bushmen of Africa have always led a harsh and difficult life and often seem to be losing their battle with the environment and with their fellow men. The background of the Zulu nation could hardly be more different; the people have had a proud history and a sophisticated culture, and it is not surprising that the customs surrounding their marriage ceremonies are complex and long drawn out. Soon after a Zulu maiden has completed the rites surrounding her puberty she will begin to think of finding herself a husband. First, however, she has to obtain the agreement of the senior unmarried girls in her kraal, who do not want too many people in the marriage market at once. Indeed the girl may have to wait for some months before she is given the go-ahead to enter stage one of the marriage stakes. During this stage she can talk and flirt mildly with the young men who take her fancy but if she wants matters to go any further she has to approach her father and ask him to hold a "coming-out" party for her when she will be formally presented to local society. If he agrees he will have a circle of wicker built and place his daughter in it while he makes preparation for the ceremony, a date for which will be chosen some little time ahead. Invitations will be sent out to male relatives, friends and neighbors, some of whom will offer animals to be killed for the feast. Everyone asked will set his women to making ample supplies of beer, an essential element in all Zulu feasts.

The day before the coming out ceremony, the girl's father will kill an animal as a sacrifice to mark the coming of marriageable age of his daughter, and in the evening the young people of the kraal will serenade her around her wicker cage. On the day of the ceremony itself, the young girls decorate themselves and join the debutante in her seclusion. They all emerge around midday and dance, two by two, before the applauding guests. Each couple tries to outdo the other in the skill and sexiness of their dancing, and the girl of the day tries to outdo them all. They dance and dance until they can do no more and return to the wicker circle where lots of beer and freshly cooked meat await them. The rest of the guests eat and drink as much as possible before the setting of the sun shows that it is time for them to return to their huts. The elders having gone, the young people then dance, eat and drink with even more abandon until the early hours of the morning.

The young woman is now free to let her hair grow, and when she goes down to the river to fetch water she dresses to kill, drawing attention to herself by singing loudly as she approaches the river bank. The young men flock around her and flirt with her and she has ample opportunity to select the one she would like as her husband. Before she can make her choice known, however, she once again has to seek permission from the older unmarried girls of her kraal. As before, they are likely to keep her waiting for several months before they give her permission to proceed. Even then matters are not straightforward, for custom forbids her to tell him directly of her feelings. Instead she must brush aside his advances, telling him that she is but a child and too young to consider serious matters such as marriage. The formula used, however, is well established and instead of being thrown into despair the young man will be delighted to know that he is making real progress. Another sign of his sweetheart's favor is given to him should he be set upon by her young sister, or some other close female relative, and be beaten with a bunch of twigs. Once this has happened he will fly a white cloth from a pole outside his hut as a sign that he has had a declaration of love from a girl.

When things have gone as far as this, the girl can make her feelings known by presenting her chosen young man with a necklace of white beads. They then have status as officially declared sweethearts and give each other gifts of jewelry. They can spend their nights together and make love, always provided that the girl does not lose her virginity, and has the permission of the senior girls in her kraal, who instruct her in sexual matters. The older women of the krall will inspect the girl at regular intervals to ensure that she is still technically a virgin. Should she not be, a great fuss is made and payment of a fine is extracted from the young man, or from his family, while the wedding ceremony is brought forward. Normally, several months pass between the official exchange of engagement gifts and the actual wedding ceremony. During this period the male relatives of the fiancé will have visited the girl's parents to tell them that she is to visit her fiancé, and start negotiating the bride price.

While these negotiations go on, the girl will stay as a guest at her fiancé's kraal, getting to know him and his people. The actual negotiations about the bride price and the details of the wedding ceremony are carried out by an officially appointed matchmaker and his assistant. They may go on for some time as the women insist upon all the details being firmly settled. Cattle, which have not only economic but religious significance, almost always change hands, as well as cash, jewelry and other goods. The bride regards the bride price as an essential part of the wedding ceremonial, and a firm sign of the loss she will be to her father. It also indicates how highly she is regarded by her fiancé and his family. As it represents a significant sum, it is also a steadying influence which inhibits the break-up of marriages, for it has to be forfeited or repaid should one partner leave the other at some future date. Zulu fathers keep a close eye on the continuing welfare of their daughters after marriage.

The departure of a daughter from the kraal to live forever among another clan is a moment of great sadness. Her father will slaughter one of her cattle, bought by the bride price, and ripping out the gall bladder he will empty out its contents over her face, arms and legs. While he does this he will address the spirits of his ancestors and tell them of his daughter's change of status. The girl is then taken aside by the old women of the tribe and instructed how to behave as a dutiful wife and daughter-in-law. The procession then sets off to the groom's kraal, with the bride accompanied by the matchmaker and the men of her kraal. The numbers will swell along the way as others join in.

On arriving, the bride and her attendant are now conducted to their specially prepared hut, from which they emerge to join the groom's party and their own for the ceremonious hurling of insults. Each side goes on far into the night hurling the deadliest abuse possible at the members of the opposite party. Morals, characters, courage, and honesty are called into question in the most offensive way possible. Insults are freely exchanged which would normally lead to physical assault. On this occasion all they lead to is delighted laughter and applause until the participants and their audience are speechless with exhaustion.

Surrounded by her attendants, the Zulu bride sets off in procession from her own kraall to that of her groom.

The next day is that of the actual wedding. The bride and her girl friends bathe in the river, eat their own food and dress themselves as grandly as possible for the dancing. They tie bags of pebbles to their ankles to produce a rhythmic rattling sound and paint their faces, arms and legs with designs in red and white ocher. The bride wears a veil decorated with a long fringe and beads, ties white oxtail fringes to her elbows and below her knees, a goat's hair fringe adorns her neck. In her hand she carries a large knife to denote her virginity. At about midday the bridal party is called upon to open the dancing and make its way to the open area, escorted by the young men of the bride's kraal with their shields uplifted. Once there they line up opposite the groom's party and the dance begins. When it is over, the father of the groom makes a speech welcoming the bride's party, praising her beauty and character and saying that she is worth every item of the bride price. The full bridal party then enters and dances the special wedding dance so that it may be witnessed by the spirits of the groom's ancestors. After this beer and cooked meats are served as the members of the groom's party go off to dress themselves in their wedding finery. The groom tops off his beads and skins with a feather head-dress made of the tail-feathers of a large finch.

When the groom's party is ready, the eating and drinking is put aside and the groom is ceremoniously seated upon a special mat with the bride, screened from view, in front of him. Then her screens are thrown aside and she is revealed in all her glory as she begins her own special wedding dance. This combines aggression and sensuality as she dances ever more wildly, but at the same time stabbing at imaginary enemies with her knife and fending them off with a small shield; this dance rouses everyone into a frenzy. Just before the bride must drop with exhaustion, her father steps forward and taps the ground. As suddenly as the dance started, it stops. It is now the groom's turn and he dances, backed by the men of his party, and at the same time sings his own praises in winning so superb a wife and gradually turning, with his friends, to songs boasting of the excellence of his tribe. All the time the dancing continues in faultless rhythm until they too stop suddenly and take their places seated opposite the bridal party, leaving a gap between them. The brothers of the bride, or her nearest male relatives, now drive in a gift of three cattle, each one of which has a special significance. Their quality is loudly, and accurately, judged by the crowd, so it is a matter of honor to make them as good as possible. Having been paraded, the cattle are driven away and silence falls upon the crowd as the bride rises to her feet and casts herself down before her father-in-law and begs him to accept her into his family. Matters having proceeded so far, the father-in-law will, of course, accept her. The bride's father will now rise to his feet and tell the assembly of his daughter's virtues but he will also mention her faults and ask for them to be accepted kindly. He will also express a wish that his daughter will prove fruitful and that she will be given a good home by her new family. He will end by calling upon his son-in-law, with great emotion, to be a kind and understanding husband and to cherish his daughter.

After these moving and very human family moments the bride and groom have to make an appearance before a government official. He will formally ratify their marriage. A great cheer greets his announcement and everyone rushes to the cooking and beer pots as the feasting begins for everyone but the bride. She has to return to her hut, remove her finery and eat the food she originally brought with her. While everyone else is indulging in abandoned dancing, feasting and lovemaking she sleeps alone.

The next morning an ox is paraded before the crowd, this time the gift of the groom's father. It has to be killed with one blow of the spear and the intestines have to be removed undamaged. The groom's party then take the gall bladder and force themselves into the bride's hut despite strong resistance from the bridesmaids. Having won their way to the bride, they pour the contents of the gall bladder over her. This is supposed to ensure that she becomes a mother as soon as possible but its immediate effect is to make it necessary for the bride and her maids to go to the river for another bath. The groom's father's ox is eaten during the day by the girls of the bride's party, except for her, and in the evening the groomsmen force themselves into her hut again. This time the struggle stops when one of the groom's party is able to strike her on the ankle with a small stick. At once she begins to sing and goes along with the young men to the husband's hut. There they are left alone to consummate the marriage. When this is done, the bride cries out, expressing grief, so that those guests who are left may know that she is no longer a virgin.

For how long such traditional tribal wedding ceremonies will survive in an Africa moving towards an urban society is difficult to estimate. At the moment many urban Africans live in a state of social disorganization pulled in two different directions by tribal and urban customs and, in many cases, having to make do with the worst of both worlds. In those African states where colonial rule has been exchanged for home rule there has not been any strong move back to tribal values. The Africans who now lead their countries have been educated in, and have largely adopted, western patterns of behavior and it is likely that African society as a whole will slowly adopt western forms of social values that will lead to the slow death of tribalism and the disappearance of such age-old wedding ceremonies as exist today.

In the Islamic areas of the African continent the pace of change is perhaps not so noticeable in matters affecting family life. In Morocco the young people now have some say in their marriages, but the parents still have a great deal of influence, conducting the negotiations and making most of the decisions. A wedding is seen not only as the uniting of a man and a woman but as the joining of two family groups. Short engagements are not encouraged and there is often a betrothal period of up to two years. A dowry has to be agreed before notaries and paid up in addition to gifts of clothes, perfume and jewelry from the groom to the bride. A marriage contract is drawn up, the wedding day is fixed and the dowry is spent on preparing the bride's trousseau and on buying furniture for the new home.

Five days before the ceremony, women known as *negaffa* prepare the marriage chamber and lay out the mattresses and blankets. Prior to the wedding day the bride goes to the Turkish bath for a ritual cleansing ceremony which is interspersed with songs in praise of both the Prophet and the bride. She then returns to her home where, behind a curtain, the *negaffa* draw patterns on her hands and feet with henna. The next evening a reception is held and on the day following that the *negaffa* return to prepare the bride. Her face is made mask-like with make-up and then veiled and she is dressed in fine brocades and jewels before being taken into the courtyard, escorted by women bearing candles. She sits down upon a table in the center. This is raised up on the *negaffa*'s shoulders, tambourines are struck and everyone sings and shouts. The bride is then returned to her bedroom, her hair is braided and new henna designs are drawn upon her. She is then seated on a throne and receives gifts from the wedding guests.

At the groom's house the older guests are already gathered and listen to music appropriate to their age while the groom entertains his young companions in a neighbor's house with a popular band. On the evening of the wedding day, celebrations go on in the houses of the two sets of parents and in the groom's own house. In the early hours of the morning the musicians and those guests who are not of the immediate family go home. The rest form a procession led by children carrying candles and make their way to the bride's house chanting songs. They bring her back to the bridegroom's house where her mother-in-law lifts her veil and kisses her in welcome. Two of the *negaffa* now go to fetch the bridegroom. He, face hooded, is placed by his bride while the *negaffa* literally sing her praises, turn her to face her husband and ceremoniously unveil her. The young couple are then left alone.

OPPOSITE *Bride and groom from the Meru people of Tanzania. It is not recorded whether the goats were part of the bride price.*

OVERLEAF *Brides of the Fulani people, Nigeria. Traditionally Fulani men seeking wives have to impress with their bravery.*
ABOVE *At this Berber wedding in Morocco the bride dances in front of the men.*
RIGHT *These camel-borne drummers formed a loud and spectacular part of a wedding procession in old Cairo.*

ABOVE *The Persian bride, veiled from head to foot, is conducted to her wedding.*

RIGHT *At a more recent Persian wedding, the guests prepare for the dance.*

FAR RIGHT *According to this old French print, the Turkish suitor scars himself to prove his feelings. His beloved appears skeptical.*

THE MYSTERIOUS EAST

"Marriage is honorable in all" HEBREWS, xiii, 4

To WESTERNERS THE Japanese have always been somewhat mysterious, so long did they close their country to outsiders. The basis of their society is also radically different from any that has operated in Europe or America for the past few hundred years. The thinking behind it is largely feudal despite the amazing pace of industrial development and outward social change that has taken place in the country since the Second World War. Before we can understand their view of marriage today we have to try to understand the foundations upon which it is based.

Life amongst the Japanese nobility some two hundred years before the Norman Conquest of England in 1066 was stylized and very formal. Great attention was given to beauty and culture. A Japanese nobleman of that time being confronted with his opposite number in France or England would have been horrified at the brutality and almost total lack of civilized behavior he observed. This approach to life is well illustrated in the formal attitude to marriage adopted when a nobleman wished to marry either a principal or a secondary wife; for a man could maintain with propriety both principal and secondary wives, and concubines.

The nobleman would approach, or be approached by, a matchmaker who knew of a likely girl. If he thought that the girl sounded suitable he would write her a thirty-one syllable poem saying the right romantic things. This would be delivered by the matchmaker and the girl, or her family, would immediately compose one in reply. This would be studied by her suitor with great care as her skill with the verse and her ink-brush would give him a good idea of her breeding and attainments. Should these seem satisfactory he would arrange to visit her secretly.

The secrecy was a matter of convention, for her family would be well aware of his visit, as would the girl's servants. Convention also dictated that the nobleman should acquit himself like a sexual athlete, giving the girl no rest until he staggered away, another convention, at the first light of dawn.

Once back in his quarters, the nobleman had to ignore any fatigue he might feel and write a formal "next-morning" letter to the girl in which he would express elaborate sentiments about the grief he felt at being separated from her by the cruel light of day. He would also send her another formal love poem. These were delivered by a special messenger and were a sign to the girl's parents that all had gone well. The messenger was royally entertained, while the girl wrote her formal reply filled with accepted images of romance, and then he reeled back with it.

On the second night and day the pattern was repeated; all participants no doubt showing some signs of strain. For the third night some small rice cakes were prepared and put into the girl's room by her family. These were in honor of the Shintoist progenitors, Izanagi and Izanami. By eating them, the nobleman and his lady performed the wedding ceremony with religious sanction. The next dawn could be ignored as he was by then entitled to stay with his bride.

The following evening, or soon after, the bride's parents would invite the groom and some of his friends to a feast at their home. This was considered to be his first meeting with them and the occasion would be marked by a simple service of purification, performed by a priest, and by the young couple exchanging wine cups three-times-three. The wedding was then over.

The reasons for the man's choice of a wife were based not upon sexual and romantic considerations but upon social, political and economic ones. Rank was all important. The true wishes of the partners did not come into the matter, any more than they did in aristocratic society in Europe, until comparatively recently.

Moving forward in time, we can look at Japanese society through the eyes of some of the first Western visitors to her shores. St. Francis Xavier landed in Japan in August 1549 and spent over two years there. He was impressed by what he found. "They have one characteristic which is not found in any part of Christendom: however poor a noble may be (and however much wealth a commoner may possess) they pay him as much honor as if he were rich. A poor noble will never marry a commoner, no matter how much money he may be offered: this is because they prefer honor to wealth and consider that they lose their honor if they marry a commoner. The people show much politeness to each other."

Ninety years later, François Caron, a Belgian-born Frenchman who was a director of the Dutch East India Company in Japan, was also struck by the Japanese approach to marriage.

These people neither make love nor woo, all their marriages being concluded by their parents, or for want of such near relations, by the next of kin. One Man hath but one Wife, though as many Concubines as he can keep; and if that Wife do not please him, he may put her away, provided he dismiss her in a civil and honourable way. Any Man may lie with a Whore or common Woman, although he be married, with impunitie; but the Wife may not so much as speak in private with another Man, as is already said, without hazarding her life. What is said of divorce, relates only to the Citizen, Merchant and Common Soldier; a Gentleman or Lord may not put away his Wife, although she should not please him, and that out of respect for her quality and his own Person; he must maintain her according to her condition and necessities; but may freely divert himself with his Concubines and Women, and, when the humour takes him, with his own Wife again. This liberty that the Men have, obliges the Women to observe their Husbands, and endeavour to endear them to them, by an humble compliance and submission to their humours, being sure else to lose them, and see their Rivals preferred before them. ... Daughters have no portions at all, nor nothing given them at their marriage; sometimes it happens that rich Parents send a good sum of money with their Daughters, upon their marriage day, to their Son in law; which present is returned by the Bridegroom and his Parents with much thanks being unwilling that the Bride should have any colourable excuse to raise her into an opinion of having obliged her Husband: The poorer sort do but seldom return these offers as needing them, and glad of any augmentation of their Friends. They have a common saying that a Woman hath no constant dwelling, living in her youth with her parents, being married with her Husband, and when she is old with her Childe.

Writing in 1921, the Rev. Walter Weston, who had spent some time mountaineering in Japan, was still concerned over the status of Japanese women.

It is probable that no people have produced a womanhood with

150

such widespread and lofty ideals of duty as are exhibited by the women of Japan. It is all the more remarkable because, as has been said, nearly all the social conventions exist mainly for the advantage and convenience of man. At times it is almost difficult to realise that they belong to the same race. . . . Add to these generally received views the fact that a wife might be divorced for being barren, too talkative or idle and that for every three or four marriages there is one divorce, the wonder of the attractiveness and the worth of the vast majority of Japanese women is all the more complete.

The Rev. Weston does go on to say, however, that times were slowly changing and that while marriage arrangements were still theoretically left to the parents, the young man and the girl had a decided say in the matter. But he may have been misled by the Japanese's own way of expressing their rather limited acceptance of social change. Observers some thirty years after him noted that when Japanese parents and children said that a "love match" had been arranged or that the "children decided" in fact, by Western standards, only a small gesture had been made to freedom of choice. A father may have shown his daughter a picture of the young man and asked whether she would like to marry him; or the parents may have brought the girl and boy together and allowed them to walk in the park or go to the cinema. They would then say "Oh, yes. We dated before marriage."

Marriage in Japan reflects the pattern of a still rigid social structure. The concept of marriage has no religious basis but is a matter of class and money. Only in the most westernized, middle-class, liberal families do the factors of romance and personal choice have any place. The normal marriage is arranged by intermediaries who act through the parents who, in their turn, seek to improve their social, economic and community status. Social support is important to the Japanese and they seek it through a number of community interrelationships. These include the family, trade or labor associations and neighborhood groups. Relationships within these groups extend outward to a number of degrees. A family whose daughter weds a boy belonging to a certain labor association will then be considered to have certain links with that association. This can bring them practical benefits or advantageous psychological support.

The wedding ceremony is often performed at the home of the bride, at night. She will probably wear a special kimono and elaborate hairstyle, often a wig. The groom will nowadays often wear morning dress or a smart business suit. The matchmaker will lead the bride to her seat beside the groom and will then take the special place appointed for him. Ritual gifts are exchanged between the bride and groom, nicely calculated to indicate the status of both, and then the young couple drink wine, exchanging cups nine times to symbolize the bond of marriage. This completes the ceremony, and is usually followed by a feast at which the bride and groom are introduced to friends and relatives.

Japanese law, in fact, requires no religious ceremony as part of the form of marriage. The only requirement is that the marriage be registered with the civil authorities. However, the effect of Western films, books and magazines and the example of the Christian churches has led the Shinto and Buddhist sects to institute wedding ceremonies at their shrines.

Surrounded by a vast chain of awe-inspiring mountains, Tibet has always been enigmatic, and the people have always had a strong spirit of self-sufficiency. Followers of the precepts of Buddha, they have turned their religious observances into directions that are peculiarly their own. While outwardly amenable to the powers that be, they maintain an inner independence that is virtually unchangeable. Like all mountain people, their customs tend to vary from valley to valley, but they do follow the practice of polyandry, that is of one woman having two or more husbands.

Tibetan wives frequently exercise a good deal of authority over their husbands. All the money which the husbands earn is handed over to their common wife. Should they need money for any particular purpose of their own, they have to persuade their wife to hand it over to them.

Tibetans generally, both men and women, marry between their twentieth and twenty-fifth year. If a woman who has several brothers as her husbands has a child, the eldest husband is called "father," the rest "uncle." Despite her dominant character and strong eventual position, the woman has no choice in the selection of her husband. She has to accept the choice of her parents. Indeed, the parents do not even tell her that a proposal has been made. It is not surprising, therefore, that Tibet has a high divorce rate.

When a young man reaches marriageable age, his parents make inquiries for a suitable bride among families of the same social position as his own, and, when a girl is found, communicate through a middleman with her parents; the parents, before giving a definite reply, will consult a priest or a fortune-teller. The whole process of negotiation is kept secret from the girl, and from the boy, until the actual wedding day. There is no custom of exchanging presents or of the bride bringing a dowry or of anything like a wedding contract regarding the property of the parents concerned. However, the bride's parents, as a matter of social convention, do provide her with all the things she may need in her new life.

On the morning of the wedding, the bride's parents casually tell her that, the weather being fine, they intend to go to the temple, that she had better go with them, and, as they are going to have a *lingka* feast, she had better have her hair dressed. They then give her new toilet articles and, when she has completed her preparations, they tell her that she is engaged and that she is to be married that very day. To be more exact, the wedding festivities are to begin that day for even the poor give feasts for two or three days before the wedding actually takes place whilst the rich give a series of prenuptial banquets that may last for a fortnight.

During these festivities the relatives and acquaintances of her parents visit the family with presents of money, food or clothes to congratulate them on their daughter's happy wedding. They are royally entertained with Tibetan tea and spirits, of which they drink a good deal, but they eat nothing at first. In the late afternoon, they stop drinking and eat meat and wheat-cakes and boiled rice mixed with butter, sugar, raisins and Chinese persimmons. Later in the evening, the guests are fed again at a dinner until they need reviving by singing and dancing. The dancing is regular and systematic, each dancer keeping in step with the music as dutifully as drilling soldiers, although their regularity and apparent solemnity in no way interfere with the zest and keenness of their enjoyment.

Towards the end of the feasting and general celebrations, the parents of the groom send their representatives, with an impressive number of attendants, to the bride's home for the bride. They take with them a sum of money known as "breast money." This is supposed to remunerate the mother for the expense of bringing up the bride. The middleman then presents the bride with all the necessary clothing for the wedding ceremony: dress, belt and Chinese shoes. A jewel is also presented and this is usually worn in the center of the forehead. The bride's own parents also give her valuable jewels to adorn her neck, ears, fingers, arms and breast.

Early in the morning of the actual wedding day, the bride's parents give her a farewell banquet. At the same time the Buddhist priests are asked by the family to hold a festival service in honor of the village and family gods. Simultaneously, another festival is held in the house of the bride by a priest of the Bon religion—the ancient religion of Tibet. When this banquet is over, a preacher is called in who exhorts the bride by means of a collection of maxims. He tells her that she must behave with kindness, obey her superiors, including her new parents-in-law, wait upon her husband and his brothers and sisters with equal kindness, and treat her servants as if they were her own children. The father and mother, with tears, repeat similar worthy sentiments, and then friends and relatives, also bursting into tears, add their own fond advice.

After all this high emotion, it is not surprising that, when the bride eventually leaves her parents home, she too weeps loudly and bitterly and exhibits the greatest reluctance to be placed on the back of her horse to be escorted to the house of her husband. Her face is covered with a cloth so that no glimpse of her can be had during the journey. When the bride eventually reaches the groom's house, she finds the way bolted and barred and it remains so until a man, especially chosen for his warlike appearance, wields an especially charmed sword that tears to pieces the surrounding evil spirits that have ridden along with the bride. This done, the groom's mother comes out with some sour milk and a mixture of baked flour, butter and sugar and leads the party to yet another banquet. Meanwhile, a priest is brought in to inform the gods of the village and of the house that an addition has been made to the family whom they are asked to welcome. These prayers over, the groom's parents give the couple, and all the guests, pieces of silk. This last ceremony makes the couple husband and wife.

The Burmese are not a race with much time for the red tape of officialdom, and a wedding is only registered as a future safeguard against disputes over the ownership of property. The traditional Burmese wedding has had no real connection either with religion or the state. Two people would begin to live together and would let it be known that they were married, and it was so. If they wished to formalize it, then they would announce their intention before someone of obvious standing, like a village headman, and in the presence of their more prestigious relations.

However, the Burmese do like to enjoy themselves. They also share the universal human desire to celebrate this greatest day of their lives. So most weddings in Burma are marked by some form of ceremony and by a good deal of feasting and general merrymaking. Amongst the wealthier families the guests are relations and a number of social acquaintances. Amongst the poorer people, the family is joined by nearly everyone in the local community. With both groups the celebration goes on for as long as possible.

On the day of the wedding, the house is decorated with colored streamers and the bride is dressed in her best silks with a gauzy, long-sleeved jacket and scarf. All the jewelry she possesses will be worn; gold, diamond and pearl necklaces and rings on every finger. Her hair will be dressed on top of her head in a coil in the old court style. She will look every inch the "Queen of the Day." While she is being prepared, the guests will be arriving and will seat themselves in two groups, the men in one, the women in the other. The men will begin feasting immediately while the women dutifully await their turn in the room where the ceremony will take place. The money that the groom has brought to the marriage will be displayed in urns and an offering of fruit will be piled high between them. On the floor will be placed two large silk cushions with two smaller cushions in front of them each bearing a formal bouquet of flowers. A vessel containing water will also stand in front of the cushions.

When the male guests learn that both the bride and the groom are ceremonially dressed they will join the ladies and sit listening, or rather half-listening and half-gossiping, while the master of ceremonies, usually a respected older man, reads the Buddhist scriptures. When all the guests are seated, the master of ceremonies will call upon the groom to enter, which he does, seating himself on the right-hand cushion. Then the bride is summoned, enters and seats herself on the left-hand cushion beside the groom. The young couple then lean forward, pick up a bouquet of flowers each and clasp them between their hands in the Western attitude of prayer for a short time whilst the recital of the Buddhist scriptures continues. The recitation finished, the couple place their right hands together into the vessel of water and the ceremony ends. The guests shower the new husband and wife with rice and small coins, for which the children scramble, so as to wish them wealth and many children.

The ritual completed, the guests spread out through the house once more and the bride and groom move into their bedroom and sit on chairs at the end of their bridal couch, which has been grandly covered with yellow silk and with lace, and further decorated with tinsel and paper flowers. The newly-weds sit in silent state as the guests file through to admire them and the bed itself.

155

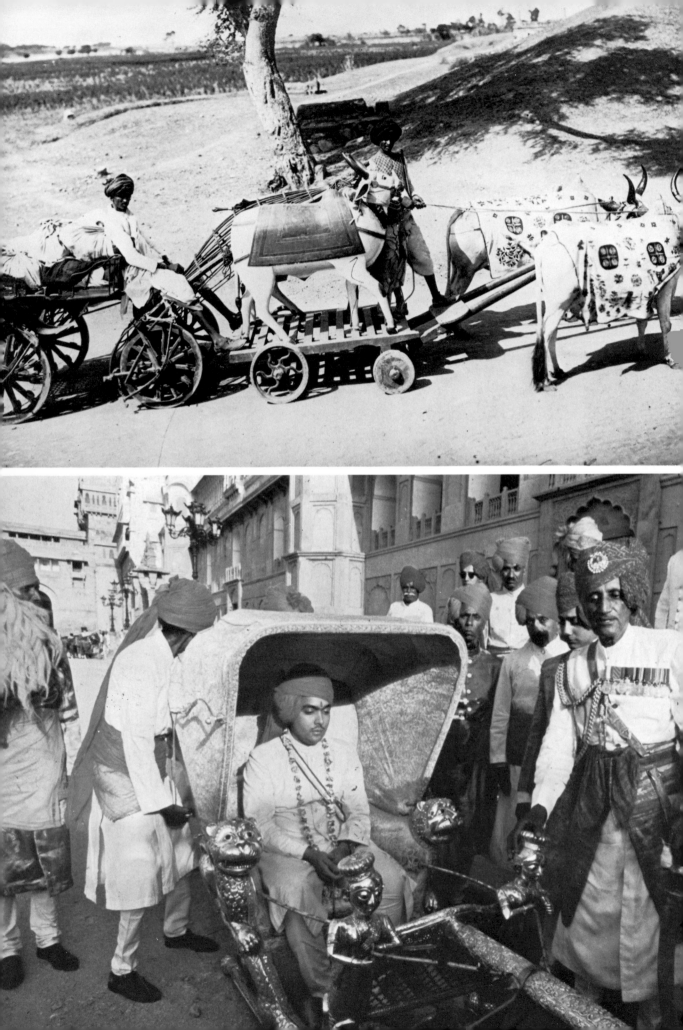

India is a land of stark contrasts and rich history, with innumerable traditions and customs. Here are just a few glimpses of how a wedding is celebrated.
FAR LEFT *The bridal couple are not the only ones to get hitched: the bridal carriage.*
LEFT *A depiction of a wedding ceremony during the Mogul empire.*
BELOW AND BELOW LEFT *Two scenes from the splendid wedding of a present-day Indian prince.*

In Laos today, young people have plenty of opportunity to get to know each other before marriage. Girls are free to receive visits from potential boyfriends at home and are allowed to go out with boys as escorts to local festivals. When the two sets of parents get together to arrange the marriage the two partners will almost certainly know each other fairly well, although this is not felt to be necessary. Marriage first, love later: this is the prevailing Laotian view. They believe that men and women are like sand and water, the one absorbing the other on contact.

Once a Laotian family decide which girl will make a suitable wife for their boy, the older relatives, both men and women, pay a visit to the girl's family. First there is general talk about village matters but then the visitors remark on the qualities of the girl and ask whether she is ready for marriage. Her mother will always say no, she is far too young, she must wait, and so on. This shows decent reluctance to part with a child, but is ignored as both parties get down to discussing the material arrangements of the forthcoming match. First there is a payment to be made into the girl's village's funds which depends on the position in the social hierarchy of both families, then there is the bride price to be paid to the girl and her parents. This is not a legal requirement but tradition ensures that it is paid at a rate commensurate with the wealth of the boy's family.

Once these financial matters are settled, horoscopes are cast and complex astrological calculations are made to select the most auspicious day for the wedding ceremony. The first activity on the day chosen is the ritual proposal. A procession is formed of the groom's parents and relatives, the village elders and friends and this is led to the bride's house by young women and girls; widows and divorcees are rigorously excluded. The procession carries along with it plates of offerings to the gods. These include betel, tobacco, cakes, meat and fish, carried in that order. Bedding is also carried as the procession makes its way slowly through the village to the sound of singing accompanied by drums and gongs. Upon arrival at the bride's house the procession halts. There is no sign of the bride or her relatives, who wait inside out of sight while some of her friends either close the door or put a cord across it. A wise man or woman chosen by the bride's family then puts quiz questions to the groom's party. They, in their turn, have selected someone with a way with words to answer the questions with such wit and wisdom that they emerge victorious from this battle of the brains. The bride's guardians then demand an enormous sum from the groom's party before they will let them pass. Everyone knows that this is purely the first move in the negotiations and eventually the groom's party is allowed to enter on the payment of a token sum or a bottle of drink. Before the groom enters the house, he will stand on a stone covered with banana leaves and have his feet washed by a brother or cousin of the bride. This ensures that he enters his future father-in-law's house pure of heart and body.

The wedding ceremony takes place in the largest room in the bride's house which has been decorated especially for the occasion. The groom sits in front of the two ritual flower displays beside the bride. They are surrounded by their parents, relatives, friends and neighbors as well as the local notables and priests. The ceremony is conducted by two priests who recite the sacred formulae in duet after passing a length of white cotton thread as a link around all those present. When the recital is finished, the guests place threads of lucky cotton in the hands of the newly married pair and congratulate them. In reply the bride and groom prostrate themselves in front of each person present and give them a gift of a flower decorated candle. They are then led to their bedchamber by a lady specially selected for her age, wealth, social position and the large number of her children. On no account must she be widowed or divorced. At the same time, the two ritual flower displays are taken from the room where the ceremony took place and are placed in the middle of the marriage bed to divide it into two. This barrier has to remain in place for the first three nights and must not be crossed. This is to demonstrate the strength of character that will be required of both young people as they resist unhealthy temptations during their married life.

On the third day after the wedding ceremony, the newly married pair visit the husband's home. The wife takes presents of clothes with her to give to her parents-in-law and to her new brothers- and sisters-in-law. After this visit, they settle down with the bride's family, for the Laotians have a saying: "To take a daughter-in-law to live with her mother-in-law is the same as inviting the devil into the house."

In the adjoining country of Vietnam the son-in-law only goes to live with his parents-in-law if he is very poor or an orphan. Even when it does happen it will last only until the husband is earning enough to set up his wife in a house of her own. The Vietnamese have a proverb also. This says: "The husband who lives with his wife's parents is no better than the lazy dog who sleeps his day away under the table." Unlike the Laotians again, the Vietnamese boys and girls lead totally separate lives as they are growing up. Only the boys go to school, the girls stay at home and learn how to run it. When they begin to work in the fields they operate in

Despite their obvious Westernization, this young Thai couple revert to tradition for their wedding day.

separate groups and if they do happen to meet even the most courageous boy will become as timid as a mouse and he and the girl will pass silently, eyes firmly fixed on the ground before their feet. Not surprisingly, the young people have little say as to whom they will marry, even nowadays when some girls are school-educated and have a limited opportunity to meet young men socially. The parents on both sides arrange the marriage and are much influenced by the horoscopes they have had cast on behalf of the boy and girl. They also consider the wealth and social positions of both families. Ideally the boy's should be richer and higher up the social scale than the girl's. Not too much so, however, or the bride's parents will be accused of social climbing. The degree of difference should be such that it is just obvious to the keen-eyed Vietnamese social observer that the girl must be highly virtuous, skilful and beautiful to have won such an eligible young man. Even if all this delicate social adjustment comes out right, however, the final decision is made on the verdict of the horoscopes. If they don't point to a long, happy life and many children, then the marriage is off.

Once the girl has been selected, the boy's parents send a go-between to her mother to sound her out. If things look likely to the mother, she will arrange to see the go-between again after she has had time to talk matters over with her husband and daughter and also to check up on the status and financial circumstances of the boy's family. If all these queries meet with satisfactory answers, the girl's mother will let the go-between know that she will consent to the match, *but*. . . . She tries to think of as many "buts" as possible, for if she were to agree to let her daughter go too easily it would dishonor her. A date is then set for the ritual of asking for the girl's hand.

On the day chosen, a set sum is paid to the communal fund of the girl's village on behalf of the groom's family who themselves are busy organizing the procession that will go to the bride's house. This procession is headed by an even number of strong men bearing gifts on trays on their heads, these trays being covered with squares of red silk. The men are dressed in long dark tunics and white trousers with black scarves on their heads and red crepe belts around their waists. They are followed by the groom and an even number of his friends and relations. At the girl's house a formal speech is made asking for her hand in marriage; this is done either by the groom's father or one of his friends who has the reputation of being an effective speaker. In reply, the girl's parents make a speech extolling all her virtues but also exaggerating all her faults, probably throwing in a few invented ones for good measure. However, they will finish by saying that in the home of her parents-in-law to be she will undoubtedly learn to be sensible, practical and obedient. After this somewhat florid interchange, tea is served and presents are shared out among the relatives and friends. From this moment on the boy and girl are considered to be formally engaged.

The day, and the time, of the wedding are carefully selected by horoscope again, and nowadays the wedding often follows quite closely upon the engagement ceremony. On the day selected, the boy's mother goes to the bride's house with the present of some betel and some pink chalk, to ask permission for the bride to be taken to her new home. The chalk represents the rosy future they will have together; its previous color, white, being the color of death and misfortune. The groom and his friends and relations then proceed, exactly as before, to the bride's house. The groom's mother does not join in, her absence symbolizing the future lack of friction between her and her new daughter-in-law. The wedding presents, however, do have a prominent place in the procession.

They usually consist of new clothes, jewelry, money to help pay for the wedding feast and always two trunks covered with lacquered leather, a blanket lined with pink satin, two pillows and a mosquito net.

On arriving at the bride's house, the groom's party finds the door closed but voices can be heard within. Before they are allowed inside they have to pay an entrance fee and will have allowed for this by bringing some money with them in a red envelope, which is handed over after a moving speech by a specially chosen orator. Once inside, the wedding presents are laid out on the bed and covered with a red bordered cloth before the altar dedicated to the bride's ancestors. This is illuminated with lamps and candles, and incense is burned. The bride's father prostrates himself before this altar and respectfully tells his ancestors that it is his daughter's wedding day and asks to be allowed to present his son-in-law. The bride and groom then prostrate themselves also and afterwards kneel before their parents and grandparents, who give them gifts of money in red envelopes. An emotional farewell scene is then played out by all the bride's family, except her father, in which everyone weeps and bemoans the loss of such a fine girl. Rather curiously, this touching scene is ridiculed by the other guests.

The procession now leads the bride to the groom's house where she is escorted to the marriage chamber. As she enters it, she has to step over a small stove burning coals. This banishes any evil spirits that may have been clinging to her and purifies her for her new life in her new home. Tea is then offered to the guests, followed by the same ritual of informing the ancestors and this time introducing the bride. No presents are given; it is unnecessary, as everything that belongs to the groom's parents belong equally to the young couple. At nightfall an altar is set up in the courtyard facing south. Before it are placed trays of cooked rice colored red and a boiled cock, plucked but positioned to look as lifelike as possible (although it has a flower in its beak). In front of these trays are candelabra, with a censer in the middle burning incense that gives off aromatic smoke smelling of aloes. The groom's parents then come in turn to prostrate themselves in front of the altar and say prayers for the young couple before giving way to a professional officiator. He invokes heaven and the two gods of marriage, chanting long prayers asking them to protect and bless the bride and groom. They are kneeling behind him bound together with a red thread of cotton which leads from the altar and around their shoulders.

When this part of the ceremony is over the young couple are considered to be married and the rice and the cock are taken into their bedchamber so that they can take their first meal together as man and wife. This is the signal for all the guests to start eating and drinking, and the men call the groom to them and do their best to get him so drunk that he must remain "pure" on his wedding night.

South of Laos and Vietnam, and north of Australia, lie islands that conjure up images of romance in Western minds, Bali, Borneo, Java, Sumatra, Celebes and many more. They constitute the state of Indonesia. The majority of Indonesians are Muslims, although a wide variety of other religions are followed throughout this very diverse state, and in different parts varying local customs have influenced the ceremonial surrounding the Islamic wedding celebration. In Atjeh, for example, the northernmost province of Sumatra, they still follow customs dating back to the time before Arab traders brought the Muslim faith to the island. Although the young people may come to their own decision about who they will marry, they do not make the formal proposal themselves. Instead they tell their respective parents of their wishes and they, in turn, inform the local headman. He, on behalf of the groom's parents, will approach the bride's parents and ask for her hand in marriage. If they agree, the headman will hand over to them a token of betrothal, the *kong narit*. This takes the form of gold ornaments and a cash payment. Careful calculations are then made to discover the most auspicious day and month for the wedding.

On the day before the wedding, the bride's house is decorated with bright objects such as gold embroidered wall hangings and mats. Special attention is paid to decorating the bridal chamber, the overall emphasis being on silver and gold cloths and as many silver trays, bowls and plates as possible. A specially decorated wedding "throne" is erected on the back veranda. On the day itself, the bride and groom dress themselves in all their finery. He wears silk trousers covered with a sarong, a white silk shirt covered with a black coat embroidered with gold threads and a fez wrapped skilfully in a silk scarf to form a turban. Around his waist, he wears a silver belt into which is thrust the traditional gold-handled dagger of the Atjeh people, the *rentjong atjeh*. This impressive turnout is made complete by hanging gold and silver chains around his neck and gold keys from his waist. The bride also wears many gold ornaments, wrist and ankle bangles, buttons, necklaces and hair combs. These add the final touches to her costume of silk trousers and skirt, fastened by a silver belt, black or red blouse and one or two scarves intricately embroidered with gold threads.

The groom arrives at the bride's house accompanied by a party of relatives and friends. There they are welcomed by the bride's party, who recite poems suitable to the day which are answered by other poems from the groom's party. This "battle" being over, the groom joins the bride on the front veranda where the *penghulu*, the local Muslim leader, is waiting with the witnesses. He will recite the Islamic creed and some verses from the holy Koran and call upon the bride and groom to express before the witnesses that they both consent to the marriage. The marriage certificate is then signed. The dowry will already have been agreed by the two families and the wife-to-be may already have exercised her right to impose a *ta'lik*, that is an agreement, either oral or written, made in the presence of witnesses that the husband will observe certain conditions in marriage. For example, a *ta'lik* can state that the wife can demand a divorce should her husband marry again. After the religious ceremony the newly-married couple are installed on their wedding throne as the center of the feasting and congratulations, so that their community can bear witness that they have officially been joined together in holy matrimony.

By no means all Indonesians have adopted the faiths of Islam or Christianity. The people on the Island of Sumba, for example, still hold to their animistic beliefs. They believe that there are at least three different worlds, that of human beings, that of the souls of the dead and that of the gods. The world that controls the conduct of wedding ceremonies is that of the souls of the dead, the ancestors of a family having particular concern as to how it conducts itself today. The Sumbanese practice exogamy, that is they have to marry outside their own clan and can marry only into certain clans, rather as it was among the early Jews. A boy from Clan A can marry a girl from clan B but not from A or C. A boy from Clan B can marry a girl from Clan C but not from B or D and so on. In effect this means that cousins frequently marry, but never people from the same clan. Apart from these restrictions, which are accepted as a matter of course, the greatest barrier between girl and boy lies in the Sumbanese dowry system. The dowry has to be paid by the boy or his father and it is normally high, being made up of horses, water buffalos, cows, pigs, sarongs, cash, ivory and gold jewelry. In some cases, if the boy is very smitten with the girl and feels that he cannot wait until the dowry is amassed, he will kidnap her. The girl's father and male relatives will immediately start to search for her, and when she has been found the couple are taken back to the girl's village and married officially. The young man then has to work for his father-in-law until it is judged that the value of his services amount to the dowry he should have paid. If the girl was already engaged to someone else, then her new husband has to work even longer to repay the dowry from her first fiancé which will have to be returned to him.

However, such circumstances are exceptional. Normally the boy, having decided upon the girl he wishes to marry, will tell his father, who will send a messenger to her father bearing gifts. The messenger will explain whom he is representing and will ask for the girl's hand in marriage, largely using figurative language hallowed by tradition. He will say, for example, that the young man "wants to have a sarong to wrap around his body." If the proposal is accepted the occasion is marked by the ceremonial chewing of betel and by the presentation by the bride's family of a sarong for the groom. The engagement is now taken as being official by the two clans.

On the day of the wedding the groom, his father and relatives come to the bride's house bringing with them that part of the dowry that is still outstanding. Prayers are said to the members of the two other worlds, the souls of the ancestors and the gods, and they are asked to bless the marriage and look after the welfare of the young couple. The groom is then taken to meet the bride, who has been sitting in her room attended by her mother and female relatives. When she meets the bridegroom they ceremoniously chew betel leaves and she rubs the palms of his hands with chalk. After this, the musicians play and the dancers dance, often far into the night. The next day the male relatives of the groom present themselves at the bride's door, which is guarded by some of her male relatives. They demand that the bride be surrendered to them so that they can take her to the house of her new father-in-law. Her relatives refuse and say that they cannot release her until payment has been made to them. Negotiations follow and finally the groom's party make a present to the guards. Then the bride, covered from head to toe in a cloth, is carried to a horse and led sobbing away to begin her new life. When she reaches her new home, however, her traditional tears are stilled as yet another festival welcomes her into her new family and her new status as a married woman.

Somewhere between 30,000 and 40,000 years ago it is likely that people moved from New Guinea to the Cape York area in Northern Australia. These were the first human inhabitants of the Australian continent and remained its sole population until the British began to settle there in 1788. It is unlikely that the Aborigine population ever exceeded 300,000 people as this number was around the maximum that the continent could support. The Aborigines lived entirely from the

With her bouquet and her garland, this woman from New Guinea shares some if not all of the traditions of the Western bride.

natural products of the country and never planted crops or domesticated any animals except the dog. They had no permanent homes but would set up brush shelters wherever they made their temporary settlements. All in all it was a hard and unremitting way of life, and one might expect that the people who lived it had little regard for the life of the spirit or for elaborate social organization. This was certainly not true of the Aborigines. They had a great affection for the particular area of land in which their tribe and their own personal clan lived, and believed that their ancestors had lived there since the time when the world began, the "dreamtime," when spirits walked the earth in a form which combined animal and human characteristics. From these spirit ancestors the tribesmen and animals had descended, and so in effect were cousins and had a family duty to each other. Men believed that not only did they belong to a clan but also to a "totem," that is a separate classification linked to a certain animal cousin and a particular area of the country.

There was a rigid social structure based upon family groups. Each individual's social position depended upon his or her relationship with every other person in their clan and tribe. The social position affected every activity indulged in. From earliest childhood, re-lationships were stressed again and again by parents until each child knew by heart in what relationship he or she stood with every other member of the tribe. The term used by a child for "mother" was the same as that used for "aunt," that for "father" the same as for "uncle." Cousins were regarded as brothers and sisters. Discipline was a matter for the whole extended family, and not just a matter between parent and child.

The relationships between people decided whom they could and could not marry. The members of a group would be divided into four or eight marriage classes, each of them belonging to a particular, separate totem. In an eight-class system a "kangaroo" man would know that he could only marry an "emu" woman, women from all the other totems, including his own, being forbidden to him. Their son would not be of either of their totems but would be, perhaps, a "wallaby." He in turn would be able to marry only a "possum" woman and their son would be a member of the "cassowary" totem. This would continue through the generations until the eighth time around when it would be a "kangaroo"–"emu" marriage again.

Aborigines did not marry young. The young men had to undergo very severe initiation tests before being considered adult. They were taken away from the womenfolk and hidden for several months while they were taught and tested by their elders and told the secrets of the dreamtime, which the women must never know. They were often marked by circumcision, tattooing or by having their front teeth knocked out. The older men would also stand around them and, opening their veins, cover them with blood from head to toe. The girls also underwent certain initiation rites but these were mainly to train them in their duties as a wife.

By the time the men had completed their initiation rites they would be around twenty-five; the girls, in their turn, would be ready for marriage at about eighteen, but might not find a suitable husband until near their thirtieth birthday. The choice of partner would obviously be limited but occasionally love would overcome custom and a young couple would fall in love despite the fact that they belonged to the wrong totems. Their only hope was to run away secretly together. They had to move to an area where their clan never went for if they were found within a year or two, the man would have a spear driven through his thigh, the girl would be clubbed on the head and their children would be killed. However, if they stayed away for some years, they could return and the man would approach his parents with a gift of food. If this was accepted, then the man and wife, and their children, would be accepted back into the clan. Normally a boy started to look for a wife in the right totem group shortly after his return to the clan on being initiated. Before he could make his choice, however, he had to undergo one last ritual. The parents of all the girls whom he might marry would gather around him and beat him severely. He would not retaliate in any way, but from that moment on he would say not a word to any of those concerned, not even when he had married one of their daughters. He might signify his choice by presenting his future parents-in-law with a gift of food, but he did not speak to them. If the girl was agreeable, the wedding ceremony was simple. The groom simply took his bride by the arm in the presence of witnesses. From then on the couple were considered to be man and wife.

The settlement of Australia, the forming of its land and the exploitation of its minerals have deprived the Aborigines of more and more of their beloved country and they have been driven into the desert regions and the tropical north but even these areas are being taken from them now; only some 40,000 of the original 300,000 are left and many of these live on reservations. However, they have been more fortunate than their cousins who formed the original inhabitants of Tasmania. They were treated by the European settlers with great violence and cruelty and the last known full-blooded member of their race, Trugernanna,

"Our Wedding," drawn by Capt. G. F. Atkinson. Bride and groom appear to be carried away in transports of delight.

died in 1876. Not a great deal is known of their marriage customs but the records of the early settlers speak of neighboring tribes exchanging women for wives and of raids when wives were captured from another tribe, their menfolk being killed if they resisted. Some kind of right existed for men of one group to marry women of another, so perhaps there was some similarity to the Australian Aborigine customs. However, it is also recorded that when the parents of a Tasmanian girl did not approve of the man whom their daughter was bound by custom to wed, then they killed her out of hand rather than surrender her to him.

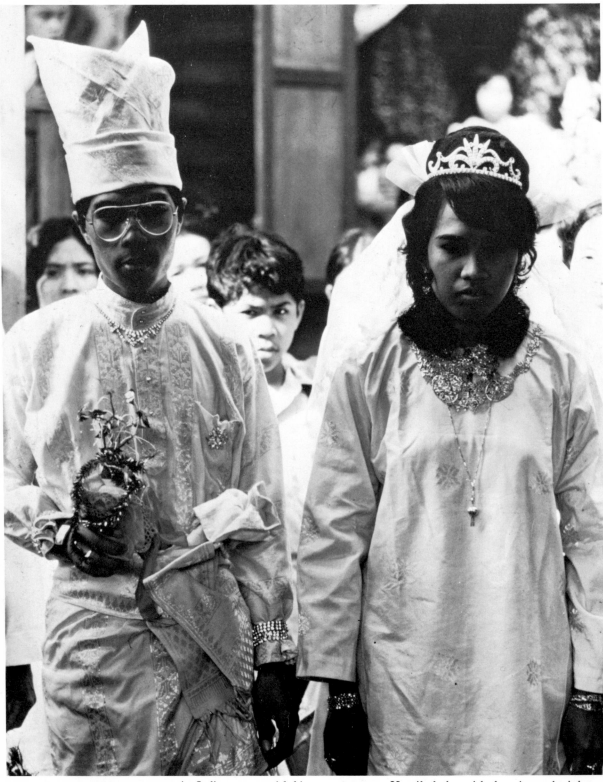

PRECEDING PAGES *An Indian groom with his child bride.*
ABOVE *Malaysia has many religious and ethnic groups.*

RIGHT *Heavily laden with the coins and trinkets which form an impressive part of her costume, a girl from the Meo people of L'aos prepares for her wedding.*

In the Far East traditional customs coexist with more modern forms. Lounge suits, white gloves and white dresses are obviously de rigueur *for the 790 couples married at a mass ceremony in Korea (above), while in Japan (right) and Thailand (opposite) traditional clothing is often worn and traditional customs still observed – as can be seen from the sacred thread joining the young Thai couple.*

TOP *Bridesmaids at a Solomon Islands wedding.*
ABOVE *At the traditional wedding of a Fijian chief's daughter, the bride is bathed inside a cloth-hung cubicle. Her bathwater is passed along the line of attendant women.*
RIGHT *Colorful clothing and ceremonial dancing make up an important part of Islamic wedding ceremonies throughout the Middle East. In Iran the women perform a graceful kerchief dance, while in the Yemen (inset) the men – and their rifles – dominate the proceedings.*

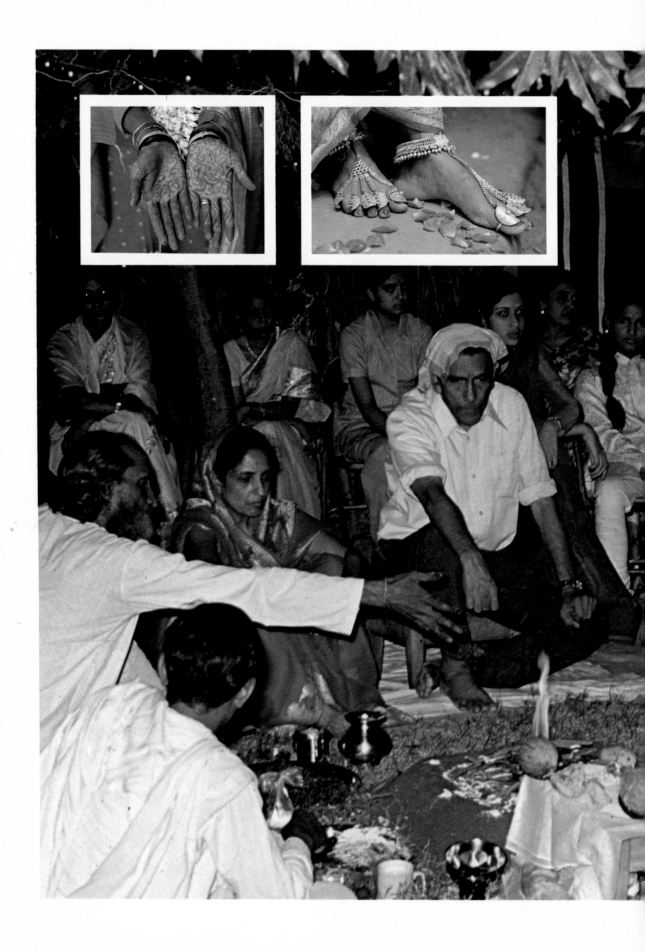

LEFT *The color and gaiety of this wedding in the Coorg area of southern India is heightened by the decoration of the bride's hands and feet. Like brides in many Islamic countries, Indian brides may apply intricate and traditional patterns with henna. This woman also wears a good deal of her dowry during the ceremony, in the form of coins and jewelry.*

TOP *The Bugti bride from Pakistan, however, makes less of a show. Aged only fourteen, she sits with eyes modestly downcast next to her groom.*

ABOVE *A wedding celebration in Burma.*

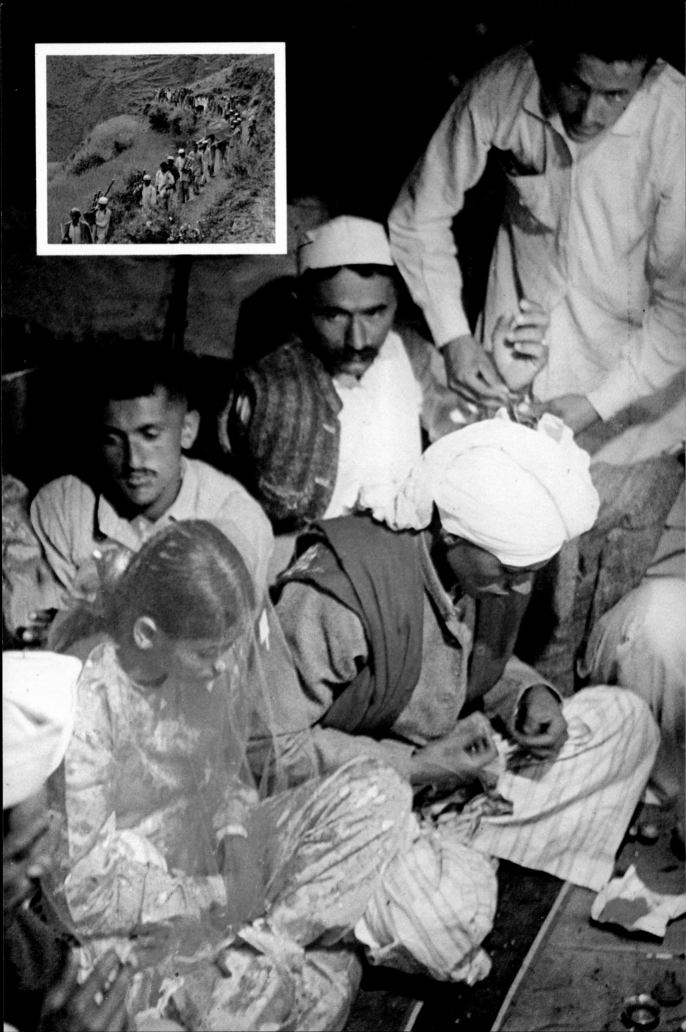

ABOVE *A* harijan *(untouchable) bride on her way to get married.*
LEFT *Two scenes from a polyandrous wedding in Himachal Pradesh, India. Polyandry, where a wife has more than one husband, is practiced only in very poor areas in which it takes the hard work of at least two men to support a family. The practice tends to die out owing to the gradual decline in the number of male children born.*

CONNUBIAL COMMUNISM
RUSSIA AND CHINA

"Marriage is the best state for man in general" Dr. Johnson

THE TRADITIONAL POSITION of women in precommunist China was not an enviable one. They were completely subservient first, to their parents, and later, to their husbands. Upper-class families paid a bride price but the bride's family was expected to furnish a trousseau and wedding gifts equal to that, or greater, in value and neither bride nor groom was likely to be consulted about the transaction. Among the lower classes, however, wives were sold publicly or even pawned, and continued to be so with official sanction up until the mid 1920s when the second Congress of the Kuomintang laid down the principle of equality of the sexes and the absolute freedom of marriage and divorce, the power of the relatives being theoretically eliminated. But traditions die hard, and a survey of north China villages in 1932 found almost no case in which parents of married couples had consulted either the bride or groom. It takes more than a political party's edict to change customs as firmly set as those described by John A. Turner, a Wesleyan missionary in south China from 1886 to 1891, and one of several commentators whose contemporary reports offer valuable insights into the life of old China. Writing on Chinese family life, he comments on the differences from the English pattern, stressing mainly the separation of men and women within the family home and the absolute authority of the father as the head of the household, to which the eldest son succeeds at his death. The mother, he notes, has great power in the women's apartments. He writes:

It is customary in the Flowery land for parents to betroth their children at ten or twelve years of age, and when the time for marriage comes, which is about fifteen for girls and twenty for boys, they religiously observe the contracts thus made for them. All the arrangements are carried out by the parents according to fixed rules. First a "go-between" is sent from the family of the young man to ascertain the name and moment of the girl's birth, then the horoscope is examined to see if the alliance be likely to prove a happy one. Should the result be satisfactory, the boy's friends send the matchmaker with an offer of marriage. If the offer be accepted, they return the answer in writing (which is the legal part of the contract), and an interchange of presents is made.

A lucky day is chosen for the marriage, and during her engagement the bride is kept in strict seclusion. She brings no dowry with her, but much money is often spent on both sides and debt incurred, while among the poor a sum is paid to the bride's parents to buy her outfit. On the appointed day the bridegroom goes, or sends a party of his friends, with music to fetch his bride. A baked pig is carried before the chair, that the hungry demons may feed upon it, and so be diverted from their malicious intentions. The bride's hair is now dressed differently, for while a maiden it is plaited, but now it is tied up in a knot, made stiff with resin, and decked with real or artificial flowers; her face also is rouged. She rides in a red gilt sedan-chair dressed in the gayest attire, while red boxes and trays containing her wardrobe are carried on the shoulders of coolies, and crackers are fired to express joy and wish good luck.

On the arrival of the bride at the house of the bridegroom, the young couple reverence the ancestral tablet together, with three deep bows; they are then each served with a tiny cup of wine, after which they retire, the bridegroom now taking off the bride's veil and mantle (which have entirely concealed her hitherto), and perhaps seeing her face for the first time in his life. Should he express himself satisfied, there is great rejoicing; the friends then come in to criticize her, and it is greatly to her advantage if she takes all this quizzing good-humouredly. As these marriage ceremonies involve a good deal of expense, poor parents often purchase a young girl and bring her up for their son; or make an exchange with another poor family for a child of the other sex. The effect of early marriage has been to largely increase the population of China; but it has also prevented a great deal of loose living, and secured the comfort and support of aged parents, for whom no legal provision is made.

Not all Chinese families of this period still held completely to these old and somewhat overelaborate customs, however. Some had embraced the Christian faith, which modified the ritual somewhat. John

High society in imperial China: wedding gifts are brought by boat while the bride prepares herself.

Turner records attending the "Wedding of a Native Christian" on January 11, 1887, that of the younger son of Mr. Lo Hoi, the wealthiest Wesleyan in south China.

At the appointed hour, the bridegroom brought a boat to convey them to the wedding feast at his father's house. The doors were open to the street so that passersby might see all that was going on, and around the walls hung presentation scrolls, with good wishes for the happiness of the young couple inscribed in gold characters.

After some delay the bride entered, escorted by an old woman and concealing her face with her ample robe, which was richly embroidered with green and gold. She wore a headdress ornamented with pearl beads, and a beaded veil. The bridegroom was arrayed in a long robe of prune silk over a padded coat of blue brocaded silk. A piece of red cloth was passed from each shoulder under the opposite arm, and elaborately pleated at the junctures. His hat was covered with black velvet and surmounted with imitation feathers of gold paper.

The young couple stood on a square of carpet before the table, while the missionary read extracts from the marriage service and joined them in holy matrimony. No questions were asked of them during the ceremony, as they did not make a personal choice of one another, the marriage having been in every case arranged beforehand by the parents.

After the service the bridegroom bowed in turn to the minister, his father and mother, and to each of the guests. Meanwhile the bride, still in charge of the go-between, was compelled to keep her arms concealed in her robe, and to wave them up and down in tiresome measure before each guest in turn while they drank tea from tiny cups. She was sixteen years of age.

Little change was noted in Chinese family life by the 1920s. Another observer commented:

Nothing indicates more forcibly the position of Chinese women than the details of a girl's betrothal and marriage. Needless to say there is never any question of meeting a future husband and falling in love. Romance of that kind is not for the Chinese girl. She will rarely, if ever, see her betrothed until the marriage. And not always then, for the husband may not even be present at his own wedding; he may be away on some business or reading for an examination. The marriage is arranged (exactly the word), frequently by some professional matchmaker and at the earliest possible age. Once this is done, the girl is held to belong to her future husband's family. Thus her freedom, if she ever had any, is further curtailed, and she is kept in still stricter seclusion. And on no account must the girl be seen by any member of her future family.

The actual delivery of the bride at the door of her future home is the crucial point of the wedding ceremony, although the ceremonial festivities and customs differ in almost every district. The wedding-feast, an affair of riotous colour, is also universal. In this neither bride nor bridegroom, although present, seems to participate. Later in the day comes the general inspection of the bride by the guests. This practice is often carried to extremes for the unfortunate girl is displayed, and her good and bad points commented upon, as though she were a horse for sale.

It is the respective parents who receive congratulations on the marriage, not the contracting parties. The girl's parents are felicitated upon having got rid of a daughter so fortunately; the man's parents on receiving extra help in the house, with the prospect of sons arriving to worship at their graves. Nor is there any particular reason why bride and bridegroom should receive felicitations, for any sentiment about the possibility of future happiness never enters their minds. At the same time, the man and woman must frequently become in time deeply attached to each

185

other, simply because of the common humanity. But on no account would either permit their friends and neighbours to have an inkling that so happy a state existed, and a wife would deny through everything that she loved her husband.

Western influence began to affect the thinking of Chinese legislators in the early 1900s, and where they felt it would help to develop the country they started to try to integrate Chinese laws with those common in the West and in Japan. In 1931 the new Kuomintang civil code asserted the equality of women as well as the principle of the freedom of marriage. Somewhat different laws with the same aims were passed in the self-styled Soviet Republic of China during the 1927–37 period. Real progress was slow, however, and on 1 May, 1950, the Communist Family Law introduced the freedom of divorce, defined the rights and duties of children and gave equal status to women. It was aimed at undermining the foundations of the traditional, male-dominated, authoritarian family and at giving women a new world of opportunity. The Marriage Law was backed up by an intensive propaganda campaign, but it was slow in bringing about change. As one newspaper in Shanghai stated in a leading article, "Over thousands of years our family relations have been that the son obeys what his father says and the wife obeys what her husband says. Now we must rebel against this idea. . . . It should no longer be a matter of who is supposed to speak and who is supposed to obey in a family but a matter of whose words are in line with Mao Tse-Tung's thoughts. . . . If a grandfather's words are not in line with Mao Tse-Tung's thoughts, it is absolutely justified for his grandson to rebel against him." Good rousing stuff, but the effect of thousands of such articles has not been as great as the authorities would wish. A report by Liu Ching-Fon, Vice-Chairman of the National Commission for the Marriage Law, claimed success in the cities but admitted that in the vast rural areas youths still do not enjoy freedom of marriage and young women were still menaced by contracts and arranged marriages. The masses still considered marriage on a cash basis as a very sensible arrangement and ninety percent of marriages in rural areas were still arranged by parents. To avoid running foul of the exact letter of the law, parents were using close kin as matchmakers, were concluding cash deals behind the matchmakers' backs or were using two matchmakers, one to handle the official marriage registration and a clandestine one to conclude the cash deal.

Despite the slow rate of progress, the Chinese authorities do not give up trying. Perhaps it is only just to leave the last words to them. In a book entitled *Destroy Old Customs, Establish New Ways*, published in 1965, the following moral tale was told.

> Recently a moving story has been circulating in Shuangwang Commune, Weinan Country, Shensi Province. It tells of the marriage of Liu Cong-fang, daughter of the famous model peasant Liu Shu-xian, to Li Hong-jin, a soldier and a member of the Communist Youth League. When the marriage took place, Liu Shu-xian did not ask for a betrothal gift nor an elaborate ceremony and he only gave the couple a hoe and shovel as presents. On the day of her marriage Liu Cong-fang rode a borrowed bicycle to the Li home accompanied by her sisters. The masses welcomed this model example of a new form of wedding.
>
> The overthrown exploiting classes are trying in all ways to sabotage socialism. They will use such old-fashioned things as betrothal gifts to spread bourgeois ideas about private ownership and self-indulgence and to corrupt the peoples' revolutionary will. We must abandon customs related to the old system and educate people who preserve such ways of thinking.

Looked at from outside, it would seem more likely that it is the people's will that is slowing down change in Chinese wedding customs rather than the subversive activities of the overthrown exploiting classes. The factors that will bring about change are education and the increasing economic independence of the young who, to an ever-growing degree, do not need to rely upon their parents.

Within the vast geographical area of Russia, wedding ceremonies varied widely according to the local religion and tribal characteristics. Before the Revolution, the Russian Orthodox Church marriage service almost always played some part for those who were Christian but the ceremonies surrounding peasant weddings would seem to predate the coming of Christianity and many of them have certainly survived into the present day. A brief description of a wedding in Georgia just after that people had come under Soviet rule in 1921 does not give any indication that change had penetrated down to the ordinary villager. At such a wedding, usually held just after the vintage, the bride's cart or phaeton was preceded by a cavalcade of her male relations, who rode desperately to and fro, galloping their horses up and down the steepest ravines, perhaps a faint reminder of the ancient marriage by capture.

A Russian wedding feast of the seventeenth century. From a painting by Makovski.

They represented the defending force. In front of the cart walked a "merryman" holding a long skewer in either hand, with bits of bread on one skewer and fragments of cooked meat on the other. At his side was a friend with a dripping wine-skin, and every passer-by received a bit of bread and meat and a sup of wine in honor of the bride.

Then came the musicians with the bagpipes, mandolin and drum. The music continued, with dancing, outside the church during the ceremony, and then the procession conducted the bride and bridegroom to their house, where the husband lifted the wife over the threshold in accordance with tradition

The ceremony described is well fitted to a fiercely independent and warlike people living in very sparse country. In central Russia, the living of the peasant farmers was by no means so harsh but the element of drama in everyday life was not so noticeable as it was in Georgia. Accordingly there was a greater amount of attention given to material

188

things by the central Russian peasant and the wedding celebrations, which could go on for some six days in all, seem to have been designed to produce the maximum amount of color and drama for all concerned—that is, the immediate family circle, the villagers directly concerned with the bride and groom and sometimes the neighboring villages as well.

In peasant circles in central Russia prior to the Revolution marriages were usually arranged. A senior male member of the groom's family would be selected as matchmaker and would call on the bride's family at night, for tradition demanded that the neighbors should not be aware of his visit. He did not come to the point immediately but spoke around the subject, discussing buying and selling or hunting or some subject equally suited to one who sought to obtain a desired object.

If the bride's family were agreeable, the matter would be discussed more openly and, an agreement being reached, a present would be sent to the groom as a token of acceptance. Next there would be a meeting of relatives and the timing and conditions of the marriage would be discussed in a party atmosphere. The groom's family would hand over a sum of money toward the expenses of the wedding and of the bride's clothes. At this time the bride's *pridaneo*, or extended trousseau, would be discussed and decided upon. She was expected to bring with her sufficient clothes for herself and for the children of her forthcoming marriage as well as bedding and some household decorations. If the groom came from a different village, the whole party would go and inspect the groom's house to see if it was a suitable place to which to take the bride.

Provided all these negotiations were satisfactorily resolved, there would be a formal betrothal party at the bride's house. In some areas the groom would ceremonially burn the girl's flax-spindle as a sign that she was to be a spinster no longer.

High fashion in imperial Russia: the elaborate headdress of a Moscow bride.

Once formally engaged, the girl was released from most household duties, wore a special mourning dress and worked, helped by her girl friends, on the preparation of her trousseau. The mourning dress marked her sorrow at leaving her maidenhood behind her and this was often backed up by farewell ceremonies and the singing of special songs that lamented the passing of her innocence. Songs played a part too in the celebrations at the bride's house the night before her wedding. A specially decorated tree symbolizing the free days of virginity was dismantled and small bunches of twigs were exchanged by the bride and groom. These were used in the bath house on the wedding morning. The bride's bath always took place at a neighbor's house and the water was fetched from a variety of wells by the bride's friends. These same friends would dress the bride ceremoniously and plait her hair. When she was ready she was blessed by her family and seated at a table with her bridesmaids to await the groom's procession which would be on its way to fetch her.

The order of this procession was firmly governed by tradition and was led by a man carrying a barrel of beer. Along the route to the bride's house various barriers would have been erected by the bride's supporters and the best man would have to bribe his way through with wine and sweets. Sometimes the bridesmaids demanded a ransom for the bride but eventually the groom's supporters would be let into the house where they would eat a hearty meal enjoyed by everyone—except the bride and groom, who were not allowed to eat before the marriage ceremony.

The feast over, both parties reformed in a procession to take the bride and groom to church. Before they started, however, guns were fired, an icon was carried three times around the party, whips would be cracked and everyone would make as much noise as possible, in order to frighten away evil spirits. At the church decorum temporarily reigned during the marriage service, and immediately following it the bride's hair would be replaited into the style traditionally worn by married women. The whole party would then return either to the bride's or to the bridegroom's house, depending on the area, and the young couple would be enthroned at the head of the table and the feasting and drinking would begin again. This time the groom could take part, but his unfortunate wife had to remain quietly wrapped in a shawl playing no part in the general festivities except for giving sweets to her new relations, who were supposed to give her money in return. After the feast the couple would be ceremoniously "bedded" by the senior guests.

Next morning, the matchmaker's wife and the best man would

rouse and dress them to the accompanying beating of pots and pans and the bride's bloodstained nightgown would be displayed as a proof of her previous virginity. The party then went to celebrate at the house of the bride's parents, where the groom would put money in a glass of drink and offer it to his mother-in-law as a recognition of the care she had taken to ensure her daughter's chastity. The party would then go to the groom's house and continue to make merry. The day after that, the bride was allowed to remove her shawl and her gloomy expression and enter into the spirit of things. She was teased and posed a number of questions and tests to show whether or not she would make a good wife. Parties would be held on subsequent days by relatives who had been guests at the wedding and the whole affair could easily take up a working week.

Obviously such lengthy festivities are not encouraged by Soviet officials with work targets to reach, but a surprising amount of fun and frolic and ritual has survived to the present day. Church marriages now are rare and the formal marriage ceremony takes place by registration at the Vital Statistics Office, while the festivities are normally restricted to the wedding day itself and one or two of the nights following. However, such features as the provision of the trousseau, the erecting of barriers in the groom's path, the singing of wedding songs and feasting and the dancing are still commonplace. A description of the wedding of a couple who were thought to be representative of good communist youth showed the groom coming to collect his bride in a heavily decorated car. At her home, he was entertained with wine and the older women sang the traditional wedding songs. After being blessed by her mother, the bride left for the registration ceremony at the office of the local soviet, escorted by her friends carrying the virgin's tree. On the way, the car was stopped by a barrier of logs and was not allowed to proceed until the groom had passed out the bottles of wine he had prudently stored in the car. After the registration ceremony the couple returned to the groom's home where they were pelted with grain. The number of children with which the couple would be blessed is said to be in proportion to the quantity of grain they managed to catch. The feasting then began with singing and dancing, and there was no restriction on the bride taking part. Communism may have got rid of church weddings but it has not taken any of the vigor and color out of country weddings.

In the cities, the party line, as expressed by Lenin's widow, Nadezhda Krupskaya, has been rather more successful. She gave the official Soviet view on marriage when she said, "Under capitalism, marriage is a business deal. There are the advantages of marrying a rich man or a rich woman, of marrying a man of position or the daughter of a government minister; getting a housewife or a bread-winner, and so forth. Such marriages lead to insecure, false relations between husband and wife, and insecurity and falseness develop very easily into deception. In most cases husband and wife have illicit affairs; men go to prostitutes. A marriage of convenience is inevitably attended by deception, unfaithfulness, vulgarity and licentiousness." In its way this somewhat sweeping statement reflects the Marxist approach to marriage as exemplified in the early days of the revolution. In an attempt to break down the rigid traditionalism of the Russian family and make way for new and better ideas, the early revolutionaries almost flushed the concept of wedded bliss away with the other old tsarist notions. Many western traditionalists feared that the Marxists wanted to do away with marriage altogether. This was not so, except in the case of a few extremists. What they wanted to do, and said they wanted to do, was to mold marriage into a new shape. Alexandra Kollontai, a spokeswoman for the system, said, "The communist system will help clear married life from its undercurrent of material calculations and profit. ... The communist society approaches the working woman and the working man and says to them: 'You are young, you love each other. Every one has the right to happiness. Therefore live your life. Do not flee happiness. Do not fear marriage, even though marriage was truly bondage for the working man and woman of capitalist society. On the ruins of the former family we shall soon see a new form rising which will involve altogether different relations between men and women, and which will be a union of affection and comradeship, a union of two equal members of the communist society, both of them free, both of them independent, both of them workers.'" Admirable sentiments and excellent intentions, but they needed to be backed up by considerable changes in outlook and in the law. New codes relating to family matters were published in 1918, 1926, 1936 and 1944, all of them embracing laws aimed at freeing the people from the constraints of custom, religion and race in marriage. At first marriages could be registered officially, *de jure*, or the couple could simply set up home together and then be regarded as being, *de facto*, married. This system did not work in practice and was ended in 1944 by the fourth Code of Family Law, in which one article stated that: "only registered marriage produces the rights and obligations of husband and wife laid down in the Codes of Laws on Marriage, Family and Guardianship of the Union Republics." This reflected a less extreme view of marriage. It was supported by another article, which stated that provision should be made for "the introduction of a ceremonial procedure at the registration, the allocation for this purpose of suitable premises and equipment, and the presentation in a proper manner to the citizens concerned of a document fittingly designed." Mankind's deep inherent need for a wedding ceremony had triumphed once again.

It is not surprising that it should do so for the ordinary Soviet town wedding had become a depressing occasion. The 1926 Code had laid down the procedure to follow when registering a marriage at the ZAGS, the State Bureau for the Registration of Acts of Civil Condition. First the couple had to identify themselves by producing their internal passport, then they had to sign a declaration that no impediment to their marriage existed and guarantee that they had given each other all the required details as to the state of their health, any former marriage and children. The registrar would then read to them a warning that they would be committing a civil offense if they ran counter to the rules in any way. If they had not lost heart by then, the couple would sign the register and details of their marriage would be entered in their respective passports. They were then married. No wedding ceremony took place and no witnesses were required; not exactly a jolly occasion and its gloom and lack of color did not suit the Russian temperament. Even the official view of these ZAGS weddings was not particularly favorable. An account in the *Moscow Bolshevik* was part of the campaign leading up to the re-introduction of wedding ceremonies. In describing what it claimed was a typical ZAGS wedding, the *Moscow Bolshevik* painted this picture:

It is a gray, bleak building. As the young couple enter, the bride speaks in a frightened whisper, "It's so dark—I can't see anything." The groom takes a torch from his pocket and casts the beam around the dingy room, dimly lighting the torn wallpaper and the cobwebs dangling from the ceiling. On a broken-down bench along the wall an old woman sits weeping. Hardly able to believe it, the party wonder if they have come to the right place, but there is no mistake.

They pass on into a second room, just as bleak and unwelcoming. Behind a wooden table covered with a dirty, ink-stained cloth sits the registrar wrapped in her overcoat, felt boots and scarf. She looks blankly at the party and says, "Next, who has died?" The bridegroom explains that they have come to get married, not to register a death. The registrar orders them to wait in the next room while she deals with the old woman. Gloomily the party wait against a background of the old woman's weeping and wailing. Eventually they are called in.

The whole depressing business is somehow summed-up by the fact that, when they try to sign the register, they find that the ink is frozen in the ink-well.

With the prospect of having their wedding in such bleak circumstances it is not surprising that an increasing number of young people dared the disapproval of the Party and got married in church. This was a trend that the state could not allow to go unchecked and so in Leningrad in 1959 the first wedding palace, *Dvorets Brakoschetaniia*, was opened in a former Romanov country house. Here the atmosphere is very different from that at the ZAGS. Everything is plush and gilt and well lit. Piped music plays in the background and there are shops with presents, flowers and even the ring may be bought. After the ceremony, the wedding party can have a glass of wine and their photographs taken in a special ante-room before moving off to their reception. The whole process is fast, they handle about five to six couples in an hour, but there is no doubt that the bride and groom feel that they have been treated as something special.

Both Marxist and Maoist thinking have tried to alter the approach of their people to marriage, and they have succeeded in dramatically improving the status of women. They have been less successful in their attempts to alter the cultural pattern as shown in the ceremonial surrounding weddings. In China the old ways persist everywhere that the party cannot directly control. In Russia they have sensibly allowed for the very human desire to surround the act of marriage with ceremony. No doubt China will move sooner or later in the same direction. Men and women want wedding ceremonies and what they want, history shows us, they eventually get.

The Chinese bride being carried to her wedding clearly found it an uplifting experience.

PRECEDING PAGES *A nineteenth-century engraving of a Chinese wedding procession, and the ornately garbed Chinese bride of fifty years ago.* **ABOVE** *"The Purchase of the Bride," a mid-nineteenth-century view of wedding customs in Russia.* **RIGHT** *The Russian Orthodox ceremony; this one took place in Brooklyn.*

THE JEWISH WEDDING:
FROM THE DESERT TO THE COUNTRY CLUB

"It is not good that man should be alone" GENESIS, ii, 18

THE JEWISH WEDDING ceremony has the longest history in the world. There have been changes, of course, but there is a clearly definable thread of continuity reaching back some three thousand years. Constancy to religious principles and adaptations to physical and social circumstances make the Jewish wedding one of the most fascinating in our survey.

When a Jewish couple come together to be married they will observe certain basic procedures. These will include:

The huppah (canopy)
The enusin or kiddushin (betrothal)
The nissu'in (marriage)
The reading of the ketubah (marriage contract)
The seven benedictions
The shattering of a glass

To make sense of these rituals we must go back to the days of the Old Testament, for here were laid down the principles which still form the backbone of the ceremony.

God said, "It is not good that man should be alone. I will make him a helpmate" . . . so God made the man fall into a deep sleep. While he slept, he took one of his ribs and wrapped it in flesh. Then God fashioned the rib he had taken from the man into a woman, and he brought her to the man. The man exclaimed, "This at last is bone from my bones and flesh from my flesh. This is to be called woman, for this was taken from man." This is why a man leaves his father and mother and joins himself to his wife and they become one body.

God created man in his own image, in the image of God he created him, male and female, he created them. When He had done so, God blessed them, saying to them, "Be fruitful, multiply, fill the earth and conquer it."

These accounts of the beginning of creation formed part of the oral traditions of the Jews for some 800 years before they were first written down, probably in the eleventh century B.C., to form part of the Book of Genesis. They show clearly that the Jewish people then as now regarded man and wife as one body—that either was unfulfilled as a single person.

In no other religion is there such an unbroken regard for the sanctity of marriage, usually monogamous. Where cases are recorded in the Bible of polygamy they rarely occur outside the leaders of the community, who married many wives either to secure the succession or to display the normal "conspicuous consumption" of the rich and powerful. For the ordinary Israelite, however, monogamy was the rule and marriages were generally arranged between members of the same tribe. Although Abraham had been directed by God into Canaan away from his own tribe and had been promised the land for his descendants, he was adamant that his son Isaac should find a bride from among his old tribe.

He sent his steward back to his homeland with ten camels and something of the best of all he owned. Under the guidance of God, Rebecca, his brother's granddaughter, who was very beautiful and a virgin, was chosen. Abraham's steward marked his choice by putting a gold ring, weighing half a shekel, through her nostrils, and two gold bracelets, weighing ten shekels, upon her arms. He then told her mother and her brother Laban of how wealthy his master was, thanks to the kindness of God who had given him flocks and herds, silver and gold, men slaves and women slaves, camels and donkeys. All this property had been settled on Isaac for whom a wife was being sought under God's personal direction.

This combination of wealth and holy approval overcame any resistance that Rebecca's family may have had and they said, "Take her and go; let her become the wife of your master's son, as God has decreed." On hearing this, the steward gave thanks to God and brought out silver and gold ornaments and clothes which he gave to Rebecca; he also gave rich presents to her brother and to her mother. The next morning the steward was naturally eager to be off on his homeward journey but Rebecca's family begged for her to be allowed to stay for a few days more. The steward protested and finally Rebecca herself was

"The Jewish Bride" by Rembrandt (1606–69). In the later years of his life Rembrandt painted many biblical pictures and portrait studies of the Jewish community in Amsterdam.

asked if she wanted to go. "I do," she said, and so was allowed to leave with her nurse and Abraham's steward and his men. On her departure, her family blessed Rebecca with the words "Sister of ours, increase to thousands and tens of thousands. May your descendants gain possession of the gates of their enemies."

As the camel train approached the well of Lahai Roi in the Negev where Isaac lived they caught his eye as he walked through the fields studying his crops. Rebecca was quick to notice him in her turn and on learning that it was the man she was to marry she jumped from her camel and drew her veil over her face. When Isaac had heard the whole story from his father's steward, he took Rebecca by the arm, led her to his tent and made her his wife. The Bible tells us that he loved her and through her was consoled for the loss of his mother.

The story in itself is a good one, full of human interest, but it is also full of information that we can draw upon to create a picture of a Jewish wedding at that point in history. It is obvious, for example, that it was the custom for Abraham's people to marry within their own tribe and that the possibility of one's child marrying into another tribe was a matter of serious concern for a parent. Abraham made his steward swear a serious oath that he would not choose a wife for Isaac from among the local Canaanites. Although the story lays the responsibility upon God for the choice of Rebecca, Abraham's great-niece, it was undoubtedly a fact that Isaac could only have been properly betrothed to a fairly limited number of girls within a closely defined tribal and family circle. This fact would have been well known to the steward, who would have sought out Laban's encampment as the most likely starting point for his quest. When Rebecca's son Jacob came to marriageable age his father, upon his mother's insistence, sent him to find a wife to the house of Laban his uncle. This interchange of sons and daughters, nephews, nieces and cousins is quite a common pattern in primitive societies, as we have seen.

The betrothal itself was established by the payment of a bride price from the fiancé, though it was usually provided by his family, to the girl's father or guardian. An unmarried girl was under her father's complete authority and passed from that to the complete authority of her husband. The Decalogue lists the wife very clearly as part of a man's property: "You shall not covet your neighbor's house. You shall not covet your neighbor's wife, or his servant, man or woman, or his ox, or his donkey, or anything that is his." Because Rebecca was under the protection of her mother and her brother Laban, we may assume that her father was dead. It was to Laban and his mother that Abraham paid the bride price, part of which formed Rebecca's trousseau. How the bride price was calculated we can only guess but no doubt it varied according to the standard of wealth of both parties.

We have no exact idea how old Isaac and Rebecca were when they married but we can assume that they were in their early teens. From other biblical evidence we can estimate that the kings of Judah married between fourteen and sixteen and later the rabbis set the minimum ages for marriage at thirteen for boys and twelve for girls. The young unmarried girls at that time were not so heavily protected as became the custom in later days. They went about unveiled, tended the crops, acted as shepherds to the flocks and obviously were on open and friendly terms with the young men. Rebecca did not veil herself until she saw Isaac and that was not an act of modesty so much as a sign that she was betrothed.

The Bible says nothing about any celebration of Rebecca's wedding, but her son Jacob, on his unwitting marriage to Leah, is enjoined by Laban to continue with the seven-day wedding feast, and the same seven-day period of festivity is mentioned in conjunction with Samson's marriage. No doubt this week-long wedding party was enlivened by song and possibly by dance.

Psalm 45 is a royal wedding song which says in part:

From palaces of ivory, harps entertain you,
daughters of kings are among your maids of honor;
on your right stands the Queen, in Gold from Ophir.

Dressed in brocades, the King's daughter
is led in to the King, with bridesmaids in her train.

Her ladies-in-waiting follow
and enter the Palace to general rejoicing.

Your ancestors will be replaced by sons
whom you will make lords of the whole world.

The last verse echoes the blessing called down upon Rebecca, still used in the wedding ceremony today.

The Song of Songs is another wedding poem, often thought to be allegorical. It is written in the form of exchanges between the bride and groom and their companions.

BRIDE   *Take me with you, and we will run together;*
            bring me into your chamber, O king.
BRIDEGROOM *I would compare you, my dearest,*
            to Pharaoh's chariot horses.
            Your cheeks are lovely between plaited tresses,
            your neck with its jeweled chains.
COMPANIONS *We will make you braided plaits of gold*
            set with beads of silver.
BRIDEGROOM *Our couch is shaded with branches;*
            the beams of our house are of cedar,
            our ceilings are all of fir.
            How beautiful you are, my dearest, how beautiful!
            Your eyes behind your veil are like doves,
            your hair like a flock of goats streaming down Mount Gilead.
            Your teeth are like a flock of ewes just shorn
            which have come up fresh from the dipping;
            each ewe has twins and none has cast a lamb,
            Your lips are like a scarlet thread,
            and your words are delightful;
            your parted lips behind your veil
            are like a pomegranate cut open.

	Your neck is like David's tower,
	which is built with winding courses;
	a thousand bucklers hang upon it,
	and all are warriors' shields.
	Your two breasts are like two fauns,
	twin fauns of a gazelle.
BRIDE	*My beloved is fair and ruddy,*
	a paragon among ten thousand.
	His head is gold, finest gold;
	his locks are like palm-fronds.
	His eyes are like doves beside brooks of water,
	splashed by the milky water
	as they sit where it is drawn.
	His cheeks are like beds of spices or chests full of perfumes;
	his lips are lilies, and drop liquid myrrh;
	his hands are golden rods set in topaz;
	his belly a plaque of ivory overlaid with lapis lazuli.
	His legs are pillars of marble in sockets of finest gold;
	his aspect is like Lebanon, noble as cedars.
	His whispers are sweetness itself, wholly desirable.

It is interesting to note how the bridegroom, obviously a farmer to his fingertips, draws nearly all his comparisons from the flocks, the fields and the animals while the bride, a more poetic person altogether, goes for images from the jewelers and the perfumiers. Such poetic fancies are to be expected from the aristocracy and from those in the first flush of love. The voice of common sense and experience takes a more realistic view.

The Talmudic period coincided with the increasing urbanization of the Jewish people, a normal trend for a displaced people. This led, as it has almost always done, into the creation of slums in the towns and too many people competing for too few jobs. Poverty and overcrowding made it difficult for would-be husbands to collect together the necessary bride price and for them to build an additional room onto their father's house into which to receive their bride. The rabbis realized this, of course, but they were concerned that there should be no dropping-off in the rate of youthful marriages among their people, for they saw the early establishment of settled family life as a safeguard against the possible loss of "Jewishness" among the scattered people. The Talmud is full of teachings which stress the importance of marriage.

"Whosoever spends his days without a wife / Has no joy, nor blessing, nor good in his life."

So vital was the continuation of the fact of marriage that, for a time, the leaders of the schools upheld the old style marriage where couples joined themselves by mutual consent using the old formula: "Thou art consecrated to me according to the Law of Moses and of Israel." However, this rather lax view did not last for long and very formal engagements and marriages became the rule. The bridegroom had to propose marriage to the bride's father, draw up a marriage contract and go through the form of kiddushin or erusin, betrothal. This was effected by the bridegroom handing over, in the presence of two witnesses, any object of value to the bride and reciting the marriage formula. This, as it were, reserved the young woman for him but it was usual to wait for a year, with all the responsibilities of a married couple but not the pleasures, before the actual wedding ceremony, *Nissu'in*, took place. This was also called huppah after the bridal chamber in the groom's house to which the bride would be led in a procession. Both groom and bride would wear wreath-like gold headdresses with the bride, if a virgin, also wearing a veil. Dried corn would be given to the children to strew in the couple's path in order to promote fertility. The actual marriage was deemed to have taken place when the couple had retired to the huppah, benedictions ringing in their ears, and had had intercourse. Then followed the seven days of feasting with a good deal of hilarity. Once again the Talmud gives guidance; "He who enjoys the wedding feast of a groom but does not rejoice in the heart of the groom transgresses against the five voices: the voice of joy, the voice of gladness, the voice of the bridegroom, the voice of the bride and the voice of them that shall say, 'Praise ye the Lord of Hosts'" (Jeremiah 33:11).

Never ones to lose the chance of debate, the great rabbis even disputed over the best way to dance at a wedding, but not all of them approved of the celebrations getting too hilarious, "Mar bar Rabina made a marriage feast for his son. He observed that the rabbis present were getting very carried away. So he seized an expensive goblet of white crystal and broke it before them. This made them somber."

"When Rab Ashi made a marriage feast for his son, he also noticed that the rabbis were rejoicing excessively. So he took an expensive cup of white glass and broke it before them. This filled them with sorrow."

These stories are often cited as the origin of the present-day custom of smashing a glass during the Jewish wedding ceremony. It has also been suggested that the custom represents the destruction of the

Temple. It is more likely that they are the cover of religious respectability given to an old-time act of sympathetic magic intended to ease the penetration of the hymen.

Weddings, hilarious or otherwise, certainly took precedence over funerals and also, more suprisingly, over religious studies.

> Once, as Rabbi Judah bar Il'ai sat teaching his disciples, a bride passed by. So he took myrtle twigs in his hand and cheered her until she was out of sight.
>
> Another time he saw the procession passing out of the corner of his eye. "What was that?," he asked his pupils. "A bride passing by," they answered. "My sons," he said, "get up and attend upon the bride. For thus we find concerning the Holy One, blessed be He, that He attended upon a bride, as it is said 'And the Lord God built the rib.' (Genesis 2:22.) If he attended upon a bride, how much more so, we." (The Fathers according to Rabbi Nathan 4.)

As the Jewish people were dispersed throughout the Mediterranean and Europe, their uncertain living conditions made the year-long waiting period between betrothal and marriage difficult, if not impossible, to observe. Gradually the waiting period was shortened until the two ceremonies were brought together. During this period various prayers were added to the wedding ceremony and a sermon by the officiating rabbi was included, as was the invocation of a blessing upon the couple. One principle, that of marrying one's close relatives, as exemplified by Isaac's marriage to Rebecca and by Jacob's marriages to his cousins Rachel and Leah, continued to hold good for Jews down the ages. The *Shulchan Aruch*, a synopsis of Jewish law that was first printed in 1565, stated positively that it was "mandatory for one to marry his niece, whether the daughter of his sister or of his brother." If nieces were not available, then it was desirable to marry cousins. This is an understandable practice in a people struggling against almost unbelievable odds to survive with some sense of religious and ethnic identity. For the richer and more powerful families there were additional elements: pride in their descent and the desire to keep their wealth in the extended family group. One way for a boy of a poorer family to marry into the magic circle of wealth was through scholarship and an obvious dedication to learning. Wealthy fathers within the pale would seek out potential sons-in-law who were known to be Talmudic scholars and orthodox Jews of the most dedicated kind. The marriage contract would be drawn up to include a clause in which the father of the bride promised to enable his son-in-law to continue his studies for at least a year after the marriage, sometimes longer.

From the thirteenth century onward, one of the few places where the Jews were able to settle was Poland. Some members of the Jewish community there became prosperous and, as prosperous people do the world over, they began to display their wealth through their daughters' weddings.

First, of course, they had to find appropriate suitors. There was a fairly limited area in which to search, for any prospective son-in-law had to be a member of the family, had to be orthodox and scholarly or had to be reasonably rich. The Diaspora had scattered the Jews, however, and travel within Europe was by no means easy or safe. Also it would not look good for a prosperous merchant or the agent of some Polish nobleman's estate to be traveling around seeking a husband for his daughter.

Fortunately there already existed the professional matchmaker, the shadchan. After the destruction of the Second Temple in A.D. 70 and the scattering of the people, the essence of Judaism was kept alive and developed further through the great schools set up in Babylon. The heads of these schools, men of great learning, were the natural leaders of their communities in religious and legal matters and they began to be approached for advice as to who should marry whom. Grateful fathers showed their appreciation by making donations to the schools or, as the practice began to extend to rabbis, to the synagogue. Gradually the shadchan became less and less like a great scholar and more and more like a peddler or strolling player working on a commission basis: two percent of the dowry if the happy couple lived close by one another, three percent if a lot of traveling was involved. Of course, in order to be welcome in good Jewish homes, the shadchan had to know a great deal about religious observances and all the holy customs associated with matrimony. Quite often he would either be a not very successful rabbi or hold some minor post in a small synagogue.

As he was paid by results he not unnaturally tended to oversell the goods he was offering. Every girl was beautiful, virtuous and rich; every man was saintly, scholarly and a paragon of religious observance. When the young couple actually saw each other for the first time, disappointment was almost inevitable. Many stories exist in Jewish folklore concerning the activities of the shadchan. One tells of an angry young man who, on seeing his bride-to-be for the first time, seized hold of the shadchan who was trying to slip out of the room. "You said her teeth were like pearls, her eyes like stars, her breasts like watermelons," the boy whispered fiercely. "In fact her teeth are like rotten stumps, her eyes like muddy pools and she's flat-chested." "No need to whisper," said the schadchan making a virtue out of necessity, "she's totally deaf."

In fact both the bride and the bridegroom would be pleased if the partner chosen for them turned out to be reasonably attractive and pleasant. Both girl and boy were brought up to obey their parents' will and the idea of marrying as the outcome of romantic love was not part of their thinking. Indeed, as we have seen, romance as a prelude to marriage is a comparatively modern idea and one of very limited distribution in the societies of the world. The Jews, as did so many people, hoped that love and affection would grow out of living together and creating a family. It would seem that very often it did so for although divorce was not difficult to obtain, it seems to have been rarely sought.

The actual wedding ceremony in eighteenth-century Poland tended to be lost in the lengthy celebrations that surrounded it. These began on the Sabbath, when the bridegroom would be called up to carry out the reading of Law with especial solemnity. His approach would be rendered somewhat less solemn by the ladies in the gallery showering down almonds and raisins upon him as a symbol of the fruitfulness of his forthcoming union. The children of the community would make his journey still more hazardous by fighting around his feet for their share of this gentle rain from heaven.

Once the service in the synagogue was over, the celebration moved to the groom's house, where everyone was entertained with local delicacies, wine and vodka. The traveling musicians who specialized in such occasions would play sentimental songs to draw forth tears and reminiscences, alternating with wild dance music to make sure that the food went down and that the effects of the vodka were danced off. If the occasion seemed about to become dull then the badchan, a professional comic, would crack jokes aimed at the families of the bride and groom and at the prominent members of the community. In a limited community very little went on that was not known to those really interested and many a painful truth was thrust home on these occasions to the embarrassment of one or two and to the delight of many. These celebrations could go on for several days, depending upon the wealth of those concerned, but the wedding day would come at last, much to the relief of the bride who had, by custom, been excluded from all these preliminary celebrations.

On the day of the wedding, the guests would be woken by the band of traveling musicians going from house to house playing a musical reveille. The musicians, together with the badchan, would assemble the guests outside their houses and then lead them in procession to the synagogue. The bride and groom would previously have appointed a married couple apiece to attend them as guides, and they would accompany the couple, separately, to the synagogue in coaches bedecked with flowers and bells. The bride would arrive first with flowing white veil and would be enthroned on a chair ceremoniously draped with sheets and decorated with flowers. When she was seated, the musicians and the jester would go to summon in the bridegroom for the ceremony of covering the bride. The mothers of the bride and groom would have ready a silk handkerchief. This would be held at the corners by the groom and the rabbi, who would place it gently over the bride's face. This done, the men and women would separate to perform a short sacred dance. Finally the wedding ceremony itself would take place. This followed very much the same pattern as it does in Israel, America and England today. It is the outer trappings that change with time, largely influenced by the contemporary customs of the country in which the Jewish community happens to be living.

In the United States, for example, the groom is waiting at the synagogue before his bride and he and the majority of the male guests will probably be dressed in morning dress, which they may well have hired from a formal dress rental company as is the custom of most of their Christian contemporaries. The bride will doubtless be dressed in a white wedding dress as illustrated in all the best magazines and the bridesmaids will wear those extraordinary dresses that only appear on a normally clothes-conscious girl on such occasions. The couple will meet under a flower-bedecked huppah, however, and before they do so the bridegroom will have taken the first step in the ancient Jewish wedding ceremony. In the presence of witnesses he will have undertaken, by an act of kinyan, acquisition, the obligations of the ketubah. This will have been done by the groom taking a piece of cloth from the officiating rabbi and then returning it. The witnesses will then have signed the document—in Israel the groom will have signed it also. He is then escorted to where the bride is waiting and lets down the veil about her face while the rabbi chants the blessing invoked on Rebecca: "You are our sister, may you be the mother of myriads; may your sons possess the cities of their enemies." The groom is then led to the huppah by the bride's father and by his own and takes up a position facing Erez Israel. If the ceremony should be taking place in Israel then he will face Jerusalem; if in Jerusalem, he will face the site of the Temple. Once the groom is in position, the bride is led forward to the huppah by the bridegroom's mother and by her own. In the procession also will be her bridesmaids and her closest female relations. As the procession advances a blessing upon the bride is chanted: "Blessed be the bride that cometh in the name of the Lord; we bless you out of the House of the Lord. O come, let us worship and bow down; let us kneel before the Lord our Maker. Serve the Lord with joy, come before Him with exultation."

In some ceremonies the bride will circle the groom seven times before coming to rest standing at his right side; the male members of the wedding party will stand behind the groom, the female members behind the bride. A brief chant of blessing follows: "He who is mighty, blessed and great above all things, may He bless the bridegroom and the bride"; and the rabbi steps forward to make an address to the waiting couple. There is no set form for this address but it is, of course, a homily upon the excellence of the institution of marriage, a reminder of conjugal responsibilities, a historical survey of the living thread of Judaism from the beginning of time, a rehearsal of all that the couple need to keep in mind if they are to set up a really good Jewish home.

Next comes the betrothal blessing said or chanted over a goblet of wine: "Blessed art Thou, O Lord our God, King of the Universe, who hast sanctified us by Thy commandments, and hast commanded us concerning forbidden marriages; who has disallowed us to those who are betrothed, but hast sanctified unto us such as are wedded to us by the rite of the canopy and the sacred covenant of wedlock. Blessed art Thou, O Lord, who sanctifiest Thy people Israel by the rite of the canopy and the sacred covenant of wedlock." After this the bridegroom's father gives the wine to his son who drinks some; the bride's mother then hands the goblet to her daughter and she drinks some. This done, the bridegroom places a ring, devoid of precious stones, upon the second finger of the bride's right hand declaring before the whole assembly: "Behold thou art consecrated to me by this ring according to the Law of Moses and Israel." The bride makes no corresponding verbal promise; her acceptance of the bridegroom's ring and of his declaration before the assembly represent her commitment.

The ketubah is then read out by the rabbi, sometimes in the original Aramaic, with a précis in English or Hebrew. The seven marriage benedictions are then recited over a glass of wine. This rather lengthy chant over, the father of the bride gives the glass of wine to the groom who drinks a little; the mother of the groom then gives the glass to the bride who also drinks. The attendant beadle then places a glass at the

At a Hasidic wedding in the United States the marriage contract (ketubah) is read to the bride. During this time the bride does not see her groom. Only after the reading does the wedding take place.

foot of the bridegroom; as the congregation shouts out its good wishes, he shatters it with his heel.

After a final priestly blessing, the now married couple are led away to a room where they will be left alone for a while. They may well use this brief breathing space before the social whirl of the reception to break the fast that they will have observed during the day.

While some of the Jewish wedding ceremony, both past and present, resembles that of the Christian community, parts of it such as the ketubah, the huppah, the badchan and the klezmer are less familiar and are worth looking at in greater detail. The ketubah is a written marriage agreement which the bridegroom hands to the bride after its contents have been read aloud to those witnessing his marriage. It is in form a legal document embodying the traditional laws regarding the husband's duty to his wife as well as those duties that recent times and local custom have added. The husband guarantees that "I shall work for thee, honor, support and maintain thee in accordance with the custom of Jewish husbands who work for their wives and honor, support and maintain them in truth and I shall go with thee according to the ways of the world." The document then details the sum of money to be paid to the wife in the event of divorce; a woman previously married gets half the sum awarded to a virgin. The contents of the dowry that the bride is bringing with her are also listed and the husband is responsible to her and their heirs for the principal thereof. Sometimes the husband could match the value of the dowry with a personal settlement upon his wife.

As divorce was easily obtained under Jewish law, and Hillel confirmed that a husband could divorce his wife at will, many religious leaders were anxious to promote measures that would increase the stability of married life. Accordingly they laid down the rule that divorce could not take place until all the terms laid down in the ketubah had been met. Very frequently the money brought by the bride will have been invested in land, stock, a business or a home and the details and disputes to be gone through before it can be restored to a form in which it can be made over to the wife are endless or beyond resolution. Often the husband gives up the unequal struggle and the family are kept together.

The ketubah also gives the husband some rights. If the woman "transgresses the Mosaic Law or womanly etiquette" in such a way as to make her husband divorce her, then she can forfeit some or all of her rights under the ketubah. Generally speaking the ketubah has helped to raise the status of women in marriage and has been a useful weapon in preserving that most sacred of institutions, the Jewish family.

It is uncertain how old the custom of writing out a ketubah really is. There is no mention of it in the Bible and in the earliest days written documents would certainly be few and far between. During the exile in Babylon, that land of civil servants, the Jewish leaders would surely have had impressed upon them the value of written tablets for legal and administrative purposes. Certainly upon the return from exile the scribe became an important member of the Jewish community. Great stress was laid upon maintaining religious and ethnic integrity and continuity through Jewish marriages at this time also, and it could be that these circumstances combined to bring about an early form of ketubah. Aramaic papyri found in Egypt and dating from about this period contain a record of the first Jewish marriage contract so far known. Among other things it says:

> I came to thy house that thou give me thy daughter Miphtahya to wife. She is my wife and I am her husband from this day and forever. I have given thee as a marriage settlement for thy daughter Miphtahya the sum of five shekels royal standard; it is accepted by thee and thy heart is content therewith. I have delivered unto the hand of thy daughter Miphtahya as money for a costume 1 karash 2 shekels . . . 1 woolen robe, new, striped, dyed on both sides. . . . There is accepted by me and my heart is content therewith 1 couch of reeds with 4 supports of stone . . . 1 cosmetic base of ivory, new. . . . If tomorrow or any other day Miphtahya shall stand up in the congregation and say: I divorce As-hor my husband, the price of divorce shall be on her head. . . . If As-hor shall rise up against Miphtahya to drive her away from his house, his goods and his chattels, he shall pay the sum of 20 kebhes and this deed shall be annulled.

Before the destruction of the Temple references are made in the Book of Tobit to the preparation of a ketubah in the presence of the elders so that it is likely that the present document has a history of some 2,000 years at least.

The huppah is a canopy on four poles under which the Jewish marriage ceremony takes place. As with all ancient customs there is some dispute as to how and when the practice originated. In fact wedding canopies of this kind are common to many people throughout the ages. The Greeks had a bridal bower, the Brahmans a canopy and in Sweden bridesmaids held a covering of shawls over the bride to protect her from

Two wedding scenes—Amsterdam, late seventeenth century, and Cracow, late nineteenth century. Across the centuries (and across Europe) the huppah plays a central role.

the evil eye. In Tahiti the couple were sometimes completely rolled up in a woven mat. In earlier times still superstition held that the Sun King came down to the Earth Queen in order to consummate the marriage that would bring forth the fruits of the earth. The Queen, usually represented by a priestess, would await his coming in a bower or closed canopy of branches and flowers.

Jewish religious leaders are, not unnaturally, reluctant to identify their own religious ceremonies with those of other religions, particularly not with pagan fertility rites. They see the huppah originating from the bridal chamber, or tent, wherein the marriage was consecrated by the act of intercourse. Psalm 19 says, "The heavens tell out the Glory of God. In them a tent is fixed for the sun, who comes out like a bridegroom from his wedding canopy." Joel 2 says, "bid the bridegroom leave his chamber and the bride her bower." This indicates that early on there was a private place connected with the wedding ceremony to which the couple withdrew. It would appear to have played an important part in the marriage ceremony itself, for retirement therein was taken as the act of marriage itself. Whether or not this was the case if intercourse did not take place is a point in dispute.

215

With the Diaspora, the physical huppah was replaced by a symbolic one such as the bride being veiled by the bridegroom or having the bride covered by the groom's prayer shawl. The actual use of a canopy is not recorded before the sixteenth century. In Poland the practice of a rich father "buying" a studious, poor young man for his daughter meant that the huppah could not be in his poverty-stricken dwelling; pride would not allow it. The Law would not allow the groom to go to the bride's house so the portable huppah, a canopy on poles was used instead, then it blended together with the other ceremonies of the marriage so that the entering of the huppah ceased to be the critical moment in the ceremony that betokened the actual marriage. To hark back for a moment to the pagan wedding bower made of leaves and flowers, it is interesting to note that in America and England the huppah at certain weddings is now sometimes made up entirely from hothouse blooms. Perhaps elemental customs change as little as the emotions of people through the centuries.

The badchan played an important role in the public ceremonies of the Jewish people in Eastern Europe. When oppressed by darkness the human soul cries out for light, sometimes for light relief. The gloomy life of the Jews, where uneasy periods of calm alternated with pogroms, required lightening if they were to feel really festive on occasions such as weddings and bar mitzvahs. The badchan was their jester and their secular orator. At a wedding he would start by giving a serious speech extolling the virtues of the bride and groom, and the glories of the married state. Then he would make a swift change of mood and mock and lampoon all those present and all they held dear. He did this by way of jokes, poems and songs. Some badchanim were noted singers and composers and worked closely with the klezmer, that informal group of itinerant musicians who went from village to village playing on important occasions. A typical group of these musicians would number four or five and the instruments they most frequently played included violins, trumpets, flutes and drums.

The orchestra and the stand-up comedian are not nowadays a standard feature at all Jewish weddings but in the United States the ceremony and reception given by some few well-to-do Jewish families have both and very much else besides. Whereas only around one percent of gentile women in the U.S.A. have their wedding receptions in hotels, some thirty-three percent or more of Jewish women do. Guests are often numbered in their hundreds, flowers and champagne abound, wedding cakes tower above the height of man and everyone eats and eats and eats.

Reception rooms are turned into wedding chapels and the ceremony and reception are all lavishly staged.

Such receptions may have full-sized dance orchestras and combined jesters and master of ceremonies. The food is plentiful beyond imagining and dressed into weird shapes: sliced cucumber salmon, cream cheese swans, $800 of chopped liver formed into statues. The drink is just as plentiful. The cost, not surprisingly, can be anywhere between $4,000 and $40,000.

However, these wedding extravaganzas represent a small percentage of Jewish marriages worldwide or even in America. Overall, the marriage ceremony represents a deeply felt religious link with the past, a link that can be traced back into the dawn of recorded history.

The cake. From a modern Jewish wedding in the United States.

PRECEDING PAGES *A Jewish wedding in eighteenth-century Portugal. With his veiled bride looking on, the groom prepares to break the glass. They are Sephardic Jews, with different language and customs from the Ashkenazim of northern Europe.*
THIS PAGE *Jewish weddings in Nuremberg (left) in the early eighteenth century, and in Holland (above) in the seventeenth century. An obvious point of similarity is the huppah.*
OVERLEAF *An improvised carriage for the bride at this wedding at Kibbutz Yotratz, Israel.*

THE AMERICAN WAY

"We should marry to please ourselves, not other people" Isaac Bickerstaffe

At the southernmost tip of South America lies the island of Tierra del Fuego. The grassy, northeastern side of the island was the home of the Ona, a branch of the Patagonian Tehuelche who were renowned for their unusual height. In the last century, their land was divided into thirty-nine distinct hunting territories, often separated by some obvious feature such as a mountain ridge. Each territory supported between forty and 120 persons who saw themselves as a separate clan linked through common descent. Marriage was not permitted by custom with first cousins and the term "cousin" was often interpreted to include any children of members of the same clan. The young men, therefore, had to find their brides from other clans.

Unfortunately relations between neighboring clans were rarely friendly: hunting and territorial disputes were common and the normal state of relations varied from quiet hostility to open warfare. It is not surprising, therefore, that the Ona were one of the few peoples in the world to practice genuine marriage by capture as a fairly normal procedure. A young man wishing to get married would infiltrate a neighboring clan's territory and track a party who were moving camp. If a suitable young girl should linger far enough behind the group, the prospective groom would capture her and either persuade her to accompany him or, if she objected strongly, would temporarily cripple her by shooting a barbless arrow through her leg and then carry her off. Occasionally a clan would be unsuccessful in obtaining sufficient women in this way and would have to resort to open attacks on neighboring clans, killing the men and carrying off the women. During periods of wary peace, a young man of one clan could visit the encampment of another and approach a girl directly. This he would do by handing her his bow and arrows. At first she would hand them to a male relative, who would return them to the young man. He would give them back to the girl again and the whole cycle would probably be repeated. Eventually the girl might herself hand the bow and arrows back to the young man. This signified that she had accepted him and was prepared to leave her people and set up home with him in his clan's hunting territory.

Lake Titicaca lies across the border separating Bolivia and Peru. In the nearby Putumayo valley live the Inca Indians. Of Quichua stock and speech they worship in temples and have an organized priesthood. They are probably the descendants of those Incas who ruled Peru at the time of the Spanish conquest.

The Inca empire was divided into four provinces, which were subdivided into administrative areas, and their whole society was organized on clearly defined hierarchical lines. The basic social unit was known as an *ayllu*; this was a group of people interrelated through a common ancestor. Everyone in the *ayllu* understood clearly how he stood in relationship and social position and was equally clear about his duties and responsibilities. There were two classes of aristocracy: members of the royal family; and "Incas by privilege," who were local landowners and administrators in areas originally outside the empire. Their loyalty was bought by admission into the social élite and they then happily administered on behalf of the Inca emperor the peoples who had been their followers.

The nobility subjected their sons to various ritual tests and ceremonies before they were admitted formally to manhood and knighthood. In order to preserve the kinship groups of the nobility they were encouraged to marry their close relatives. This was not permitted among the common people—indeed it was an offense punishable by death. Though the ordinary men and women were obliged to marry within their own kinship group, the cousinship had to be distant.

The young men of ordinary descent usually married in their mid-twenties, while the girls married at an earlier age, usually between fifteen and twenty. Once a year the local administrator, the *curaca*, would summon before him all the marriageable young people of his district. A member of the Inca nobility would also be present and he would call up before him any members of his lineage who were to be married. In turn, he would take each couple by the hands and join them in a handclasp. The *curaca* would do the same for all those couples not of noble descent. The young couples were then known to be betrothed and to have the state's permission to marry.

The next day, the groom, accompanied by his parents, would go to the bride's house to fetch her. When they had been made welcome, the groom would bind himself to his bride by placing on her foot a sandal. If she was a virgin, this would be made of white wool; if not, then it was fashioned out of ichu grass. Then he would take her by the hand and lead her back to his parents' house, the couple being exhorted by both families. Once there it was his turn to receive a gift from his bride. She would give him a woolen shirt and a piece of jewelry which he would instantly put on. They would then sit patiently until nightfall listening to good advice from their respective parents as to how to conduct themselves toward each other and the world. The day ended with as elaborate a feast as his family could afford, and the young couple would receive presents from those attending. The next day they would set up their home together in a house especially built for them by the rest of their immediate community, which also provided them with farming land from which to earn their living. Although the man was considered an adult from the day of his wedding, the emperor decreed that he should have one wedding present from the all-powerful state—one year free of tax.

Although the empire of the Incas was highly organized and represented a developed civilization it was by no means so civilized as the Aztec empire that flourished in Mexico in the fifteenth and sixteenth centuries. By the time they came to marriageable age, all the young people of Mexico had been educated extensively and were ready to take their place in society. This was organized on a clan basis and everyone in even the largest clan was held to be related. A bride, therefore, had to be found from outside the clan. It might be that the young man's eye had already settled on such a girl but it is more likely that the bride would have been chosen by his parents. The provisional choice having been made, the priests of the clan would be consulted. They, in turn, would consult the Book of Fate which contained a count of the 260 days in the sacred calendar, with the astrological conjunctions of the stars and planets that showed whether a particular day was lucky or unlucky. The birthdates of the girl and boy would be compared to see if they were harmonious. If they were, then the next step could be taken. This was the request made to the senior tutor at the boy's school for him to be freed from his obligations to his teachers and fellow pupils. The boy's family would arrange a feast at which the tutor would be the guest of honor. When everyone was well fed, the boy's father and the elders of his clan would produce an ax of polished stone and ask the tutor formally to release the boy so that he might marry. Like most teachers, the tutor would not lose such an opportunity to exhort his pupil to lead a life worthy of his masters, their teaching and his fellow pupils, but at length

An Aztec wedding, seen through European eyes. Whether or not merely inventions of the artist, the bride's veil and the knot joining the couple are interesting features.

he would finish and accept the ax, signifying the severing of the bonds that bound the young man to his childhood.

The way was now open for an approach to be made to the father of the girl. Two old women would be entrusted with this task and they would be given gifts to present to the father so that they might be made welcome. Despite this, and the honeyed words of the old women, the answer would always be no. Custom demanded it. Bearing still more valuable gifts and using still sweeter words, the old women would return to the attack in a day or two, only to meet with failure once again. This ritual would be repeated several times before the girl's parents, still affecting amazement that any nice young man could be interested in a girl so lazy and stupid, would reluctantly allow themselves to be persuaded to consult the members of their clan on the matter. The permission of the girl's clan having been obtained, the soothsayers were once again consulted, and they advised the parents on the most auspicious day for the wedding ceremony.

This took place at night at the groom's house, but the celebrations started earlier at the home of the bride's parents. There was a banquet at midday to which wedding presents were brought by the married women. In the afternoon the bride was bathed and had her hair washed and arranged before she was dressed in heavily embroidered garments, with her legs and arms decorated with red feathers.

When she was ready, she was visited by senior members of the groom's family who commiserated with her at having to leave her parent's home, and who promised to make her welcome in her new family. As night fell, the groom's family escorted the bride to her new home. She was carried on the back of an old woman and surrounded by torches, friends, relatives and well-wishers. The groom greeted her at the door of her new home bearing a censer and she received another one at the threshold. Before entering the new home, they each purified the other with wafts of incense.

The actual wedding ceremony took place by the family fireside. Two mats were placed side by side and the bride and groom were seated upon them. The groom's mother then gave her future daughter-in-law a gift of new clothes while the bride's mother gave the groom a similar present. After this the two old women who had arranged the marriage stepped forward and tied the cloaks of the bride and groom together. From that moment on they were united in matrimony. Their first act as man and wife was to share a maize cake with each other. They then had to sit in silence as the elders, ever eager to instruct the young, gave them the benefit of their years of experience. When these lengthy exhortations were at last finished, the young couple separated for four days of isolated fasting and prayer. After that period of purification and dedication they joined each other again and consummated their marriage on a bed put together from piled mats, interleaved with feathers and pieces of jade. These objects were used as sympathetic magic to ensure the birth of many children, who would be known affectionately while they were growing up as "fine feathers" and "precious jewels." After their first night together, the young couple had a ritual bath and were blessed and purified by a priest sprinkling them with holy water. They were then ready to start life together as man and wife.

The Indian population of America first came to the continent some 20,000 years ago across the Bering Straits from Asia. Gradually they filtered down from north to south settling the land as they went and displaying extreme diversity of life style and social organization. When the first European colonists began to settle along the eastern seaboard, there were probably about a million American Indians living north of Mexico and they were divided into some 400 separate tribes. Much of

"The Indian Bride."

the pattern of their lives was dictated by the physical circumstances of the area in which they had settled. Miserable poverty was the lot of the Shoshone who lived in the Great Basin area where the States of Oregon, Idaho, Nevada, Utah and Wyoming now come together. It is a dry area of poor soil that supported few plants and therefore few animals. It resembles the desert areas of Australia, and there is a great deal of similarity between the life styles of the Shoshone and certain tribes of Australian aborigine. Neither planted crops, both used digging sticks to grub for roots, both got such meat as they could from the scarce small game of their areas and from local insects. Both had to move frequently to follow water and the movements of the game, and thus had no permanent dwellings. Interdependence was essential to survival. The basic social unit of the Shoshone was the family—man, wife, children. The family unit was linked loosely to some form of tribal organization through marriage. The wider these links were the better, for in times of great shortage the family could move into other tribal areas some distance away and claim support from their relatives by marriage. The Shoshone therefore married outside their own group and aimed at creating new kinship groups whenever possible. Living the basic life they did, they married not for romantic reasons but for survival. Romantic love was not unknown to them, however; they regarded it as a type of mental delusion, something to be shunned and yet pitied, an emotion that prevented the sufferer from pursuing a rational existence.

Totally different was the life of those Indian tribes who had settled along the northwest coast. They harvested the sea and became ever wealthier through the apparently unending supply of salmon, cod, halibut, sea lions, whales and sea otters. As their wealth grew so did the complexity of their social organization. Marriage among these tribes was not a question of survival but of social prestige. The boy and girl concerned had little to say in the matter, which was arranged by their parents, the betrothal often taking place soon after birth and being marked by an extensive exchange of gifts which would have to be repaid in the event of the engagement not leading to a wedding.

The boys got married around their seventeenth or eighteenth year, the girls at fourteen or fifteen. Little spiritual significance was given to a wedding, it was very much a commercial transaction whereby the husband paid so much for a wife and the religious rites she would perform, mainly dances. The payment would be made in the form of a number of feasts. The financial value of these was known exactly and the bride's relatives repaid them over the years that followed by giving feasts in return. Every child that the wife bore added interest to the husband's original investment but eventually the wife's relatives would have repaid all the original bride price together with the additional sums owing on the children. In theory, the wife could then leave her husband, a free woman. To prevent this happening, her husband would put her relatives into his debt again by giving presents to her family.

The Indian tribe who lived in the area of New York State, the Iroquois, were totally dominated by their women. All property and goods were inherited through the female line. A young man's mother decided when the time had come for him to marry, chose his bride for him and arranged the match with the girl's mother. Neither the boy nor the girl had any say in the matter. The two mothers would exchange food and gifts and the young man would be told to move into the girl's family hut, so that they could begin living together as man and wife. At no time were the fathers of the young couple even consulted.

Women held an equally strong position among the Pueblo Indians of Arizona and New Mexico, the Hopi and the Zuni. They are village, *pueblo*, based communities whose houses are traditionally built of stone or of sunbaked clay bricks. They are several stories high and some have no doors, being entered by means of a ladder from a flat roof. It is on this roof that much of the family life is conducted and where the all-important stones for grinding maize, or Indian corn, are kept.

Both boys and girls among the Hopi have to undergo initiation rituals to mark the passage from childhood to adulthood. Indians recognize the traumas of adolescence and these rituals are aimed at smoothing out the problems of this period. The girls, in whom the future of their family resides, have a final ritual when they go to the house of their father's eldest sister. There the girl will hide from the sun for four days, fasting and grinding corn from dawn to dusk. This will, in future, be her hardest and most essential task and she has to show that she can handle it. On the morning of the fifth day she rises before dawn and goes out to a cliff edge where she makes an offering of cornmeal to the rising sun, whom she begs to give her the necessary strength for her household duties, and luxuriant hair so that she may be accounted a beauty. She then returns to her aunt's house, where the women will give her a new name to celebrate her rebirth with a feast. To mark her new status, her hair is dressed in a fashion known as "squash blossoms," signifying her burgeoning fruitfulness.

The young men have a final initiation ceremony whereby they are admitted to one of the four secret societies of the Hopi men and learn the secret rituals of their religion. Now both boys and girls are ready for marriage and the negotiations between the families begin. In a society where women have all the real power, it is not surprising that a Hopi girl can take the initiative. She does this by sending the young man of her choice a gift of thin cornmeal biscuits called *piki*. If he eats them, then he has accepted her proposal. If she is then seen combing his hair in public, the village can take it that an engagement has been announced. This apparent independence only goes so far however. The clan has to approve the marriage and it is the clan that sees that everything is done as it should be. A Hopi wedding is a lengthy affair involving a number of separate ceremonies stretching out over a year.

The first step in these ceremonies is for the bride to pay a formal visit to the house of the groom's family. She will take with her a tray of cornmeal cakes and she will spend two days endlessly grinding corn. On the third day, still grinding, she will be visited by the women of her father's clan who will bring trays of ready-ground meal to swell out those she already has on display. Later that day the groom's aunts visit the unfortunate girl and mock and belittle her vigorously, interrupting her domestic duties and generally making her life miserable. They do this because she is "stealing their sweetheart away." The next day is a better one for her although it starts early. She has to get up before dawn and make *piki*, and while they are baking she and the groom have their heads washed to purify them for the next stage. Hair dressed and *piki* ready, the young couple go out to salute the rising sun, to which they make an offering of cornmeal. On their return, the whole village is invited to the first of the wedding feasts. After this, the groom's family bring her raw cotton and she gives them a gift of cornmeal. The men of the groom's clan then take the cotton from the bride, prepare it and weave it into a ceremonial blanket and robe. They also prepare other clothes for her over a period of weeks. For all this time, the bride remains with the groom's household grinding corn for all she's worth. When, at last, the clothes are ready, they are presented to her and she is conducted to her mother's house in procession. Gifts of food are exchanged between the two families and the bride is left in her mother's house, where a room may have been added for her and her husband. He will join her that evening and symbolizes his becoming a member of that household the next morning by hauling a load of wood for her. When the women of the bride's household have ground enough cornmeal, they give a wedding feast in their turn, the final ritual of the Hopi wedding ceremony.

In the far north of the American continent live the people we know as Eskimos, who came to the continent some 18,000 years after the Indians. They call themselves simply *inuit*, men—an approach to personal identity as basic as their approach to life has to be. For six to nine months of the year their land is covered with snow, and frozen solid. They cannot grow food and the only wood available to them is driftwood. They live on the flesh of fish, caribou, seal, musk oxen, bear, hare and marmot. Despite the climate and the shortage of nearly all raw materials they have evolved a satisfactory way of life, for they are a people of ingenuity and endurance coupled with a highly developed sense of humor. Few people in the world make better or fuller use of what their environment offers them. They have to move frequently to keep up with the migrating animals in the spring and summer while winter conditions compel them to gather together in small, self-supporting groups depending for fresh food almost entirely on seals. Food is shared in common and they have no concept of land belonging to an individual or a group. They have very few personal possessions and live in single-room houses. There is no real social unit except for the family, although the group of families that comes together in the winter, usually no more than a dozen, will ask the advice and follow the lead of that man they think the most sensible. The tasks of the family are divided between men and women. The men hunt and build the home, the women cook, dress skins and make food. They are wholly interdependent.

Because of this very real interdependence, marriage is essential to the Eskimo. Celibacy is unknown and widows and widowers remarry as soon as possible except when too old; then the surviving partner has to rely on relatives for food and shelter. The Eskimo man finds a wife as soon as he is old enough to provide for her. He chooses her, she accepts and they set up house together. No elaborate ceremonies, no dowry, except for a cooking-pot. Among the Eskimos of the Coppermine River area of Canada, a period of trial marriage sometimes takes place, the young man living with and helping to support the girl's family for about a year. If they get on well together, then the marriage will continue. If not, they will go their separate ways and marry someone else. Any child of the trial union will stay with the girl's family, with no shame attached to it.

In order to increase their chances of survival, Eskimo men will often form hunting partnerships in which they, and their families, share in the proceeds of each hunt. If one is ill, then the other supports his family. If the wife of the man going on a hunting expedition is ill, then his partner will lend him his wife for the duration of the trip. This is not

233

primarily to supply his sexual needs, although those needs will be met, but rather to keep him fed, clothed and warm so that he can hunt effectively. Wives may be lent to other men in the group on occasions and this always creates between the two men concerned a special bond and is an earnest of mutual help in the future.

Generally, however, Eskimo husbands and wives live together in harmony bound not by a religious ceremony but by the necessity for mutual support so that they may jointly ensure the continued well-being of their family. In the long run, marriage depends on the family and the family depends on itself.

The Eskimo and the Hopi still basically live today very much as they did five hundred years ago. Not so the members of most of the other Indian nations. They have largely been destroyed by the new Americans who began to arrive from Europe in the sixteenth and seventeenth centuries. The first of these settlers were largely from England and were driven to settle these new lands in hope of profit, or of religious toleration. By and large they were people of strong character, fully prepared to make a new life in hard and strange circumstances. These circumstances often militated against the patterns of social behavior that had been established in the Europe the settlers had left behind. In Europe the Church was a powerful influence and society was organized in a very hierarchical manner; everyone knew their place and the Church taught them to accept that place because God had so ordained it. Except in one or two large towns people also owed loyalty and respect to their families and to their immediate circle of friends and neighbors. All these intermeshing social circles called for and gave support to a steady pattern of social behavior based on obedience to the head of the family, the local nobility, the king and, finally, to God.

Families uprooted from these stabilizing factors came under a variety of psychological pressures as well as those pressures resulting from trying to make a living in an untamed country peopled by hostile natives. Husbands and wives were thrown back upon themselves and had no other members of their extended family to call upon, while the nearest neighbor might be half a day's journey away. Priests were few and far between and in the nonconformist colonies, the wedding ceremony had ceased to have a religious significance; it was purely a civil ceremony. This gradually became the general American view as a dependence on the laws of God began to be exchanged for a reliance upon the laws of men. Expanding countries need expanding populations to exploit them, however, and although wedding ceremonies might only

234

"The Shipload of Wives," perhaps another cause for thanksgiving for these early American settlers.

be a matter of legal contract, or even be dispensed with altogether, married life and children were a necessity just as they were for the Shoshone and the Hopi. Benjamin Franklin wrote a pamphlet in 1751 entitled *Observations Concerning the Increase of Mankind, Peopling of Countries, etc.* He pointed out that in a country where land was cheap and readily available, a man could establish himself and raise a family at an early age. He estimated that whereas most families in Europe had four children, American families would average out at eight children. Half of those, he thought, would grow up and marry at twenty. If matters went as he calculated, then the American population would double every twenty years. He was not far wrong, although not all Americans married quite so early as he anticipated. Both the rich and the poor tended to delay marriage until their mid-twenties but all classes had large families, the average number being seven. In those areas that had been colonized earliest, family life became settled by the late eighteenth century and wedding ceremonies began to reflect the European pattern, particularly among the wealthier classes. Later, the increasing flood of immigrants from Europe brought with them the wedding customs of their own cultures but they did not always survive the impact of the much more freely structured American society.

ABOVE *Haiti, 1949. The newlyweds pose in their wedding finery before their horseback journey home.*
RIGHT *Two depictions of American weddings, widely separated in time but equal in charm: the simple gaiety of this country wedding scene by Grandma Moses contrasts with an Aztec artist's intention of recording the wedding between two important families.*

OVERLEAF *These old American lantern slides illustrate an obviously romantic and sentimentalized attitude to marriage, but a newer, more humorous attitude too, adopted by young people at this period in rebellion to the formality of their parents.*

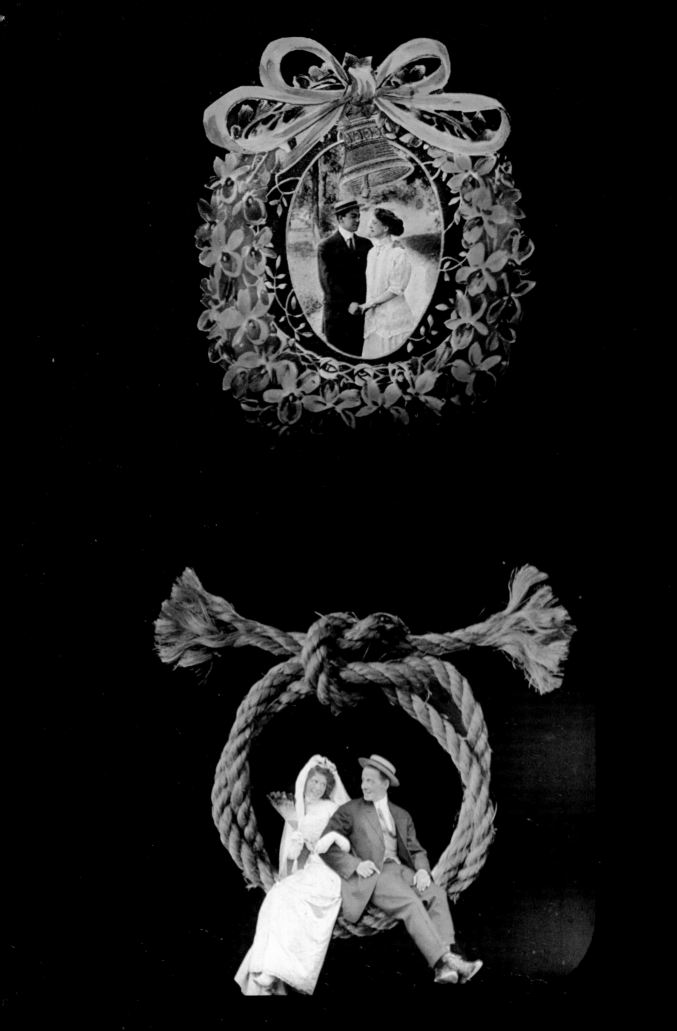

LEFT The Marriage License, *by Norman Rockwell.*
Perhaps America's best-loved artist, he captured the
essence of small-town America.

ABOVE *A few decades on, and though the style has*
changed, the feelings clearly have not.

A German radical, Karl Griesinger, came to America after being jailed by his government for his too liberal opinions, a common enough happening in Europe in the 1840s. He thought to find real democracy in action, and he did. It proved to be a little too democratic for his taste. The state of the marriage market particularly upset him as can be seen from his book *Lebende Bilder aus Amerika*, published in 1858.

A man who marries in Germany knows not his bride alone; he knows also her brothers and sisters, her parents and grandparents, her uncles and aunts, and her whole line of descent to the third or fourth generation. He knows how the girl was brought up, the nature of her environment and relations, and the circumstances under which she lives. He knows the condition of her father; all the intricacies of inheritance and reversion are arranged in advance. The young pair can set forth on their life's journey with everything adjusted beforehand, children and deaths excepted.

How far different in America! The American is abrupt; he has no time to beat around the bush. He meets a girl in a shop, in the theater, at a ball, or in her parents' home. He needs a wife, thinks this one will do. He asks the question, she answers. The next day they are married and then proceed to inform the parents. The couple do not need to learn to know each other; that comes later. . . . In the last resort, you will be satisfied to drift into a marriage bureau and pay your half-dollar for a glimpse of the feminine daguerreotypes on display there. Or better still, you advertise in the papers. A hundred to one, you get a dozen answers.

Herr Griesinger's cynicism suggests some bitter experiences in his American travels, but what he says does give us an insight into some of the problems facing the newly arrived immigrant in the U.S.A. To the shock of leaving home were added the traumas of a horrific sea voyage and arrival in a totally alien community. No wonder the first generation clung to each other and to their old customs. Not so their children however; they were determined to escape and become not Germans, Spaniards, or Italians, but Americans.

One "immigrant lad" who did marry well was Algernon Sartoris, a young Englishman, who married Nellie, the daughter of President Ulysses S. Grant in 1874 in the East Room of the White House. The service was conducted by the Minister of the Metropolitan Methodist Church and the bride was dressed in a white satin gown with bustle, trimmed with lace, orange blossom and miniature oranges. No wonder it cost $5,000. She was escorted by eight bridesmaids also dressed in white, four of whom carried pink bouquets and four blue. The bridegroom, not to be outdone, also carried a bouquet of pink and white proclaiming the single word "Love." After the ceremony, the 200 guests sat down to a seven-course wedding breakfast including soft crabs on toast, chicken, woodcock, snipe, strawberries and cream, gateaux and punch. The wedding cake dominated the tables in the State Dining Room. White satin streamers led from it to bowls of flowers which bristled with flags bearing loyal messages of a more political than marital nature. The young couple had a special Pullman carriage, heavily decorated with flowers and the flags of their two countries, to take them on the first stage of their honeymoon journey to England via New York.

However, not many young men could succeed by marrying into the upper-class society of America. Neither was that the way to success for many young American women either. Rich families such as the Vanderbilts and their friends tended to go to Europe for brides for their sons and heirs; new wealth bought old blood or, in the case of the daughters of the rich, old titles. Family alliance between the Vanderbilts and the ancient house of the Dukes of Marlborough was achieved at the cost of some $10 million.

Let us trace the procedures that an ordinary middle-class bride in the United States will probably follow today. First, of course, girl has to meet boy. He is taken home to meet the folks and then proposes marriage, and the planning for W-Day begins. First the ring. The young couple will shop together. Gold or platinum are the most commonly selected metals with diamonds the most popular stone for engagement rings, although sapphires, rubies and emeralds are also popular.

Now the engagement can be announced at the first of the many parties that will surround the wedding. The bride's parents will ask a mixture of old and young friends for cocktails, a buffet supper or a barbecue. The next day the engagement will be announced to the world in general through the society columns in the newspapers of the couple's home towns. That out of the way, the bride and groom have to decide when, where and how they are to be married and who is to come to the wedding: just family, family plus friends, all dad's business contacts? Who is to be best man, maid of honor, bridesmaid, usher, flower girl and ring bearer? All these questions must be answered in a way that pleases the bride and groom, and their families as far as possible, and that doesn't ruin the bride's family financially.

This done, the bride and groom will probably be consulting the clergy member who is going to marry them. If the bride and groom are of different faiths, they have to decide which faith to be married in or they may persuade their clergy to take part in a mixed ceremony. Their clergy will explain to them their roles in the wedding service and will describe the procedures to be followed; between them they will settle on a day. Wedding invitations will now need to be printed, or better still engraved. These invitations will be sent out about one month before the actual date of the wedding against a typewritten list of all the guests whom it has been decided must be invited; against this list replies will be checked. In return for the invitations will come wedding presents. A sensible bride will keep a card index of all gifts received against the full name, address and relationship of the donor, as well as the shop at which it was bought if possible. This helps her thank her present-givers properly and also allows her to exchange duplicated gifts quietly after the honeymoon.

As the wedding day gets closer, her friends will give bridal showers for her. At these, groups of friends will come together for coffee and cake or cocktails and canapés and will bring with them gifts intended to help the young couple set up home, such as oven-proof dishes, brushes, recipe books or bar accessories. These are given in addition to wedding presents. Closer to the wedding day the bride will give a luncheon party for the bridesmaids at which they will view the wedding presents and have the final fittings for their dresses. A pink lady's cake is served as dessert at such a luncheon with a ring baked inside it. The bridesmaid lucky enough to find it in her serving is traditionally supposed to be the next to marry. The groom will also give a party for his best man and ushers as well as other men friends. This is likely to be a much less delicate affair and it is wise to make sure that it does not take place on the day immediately before the ceremony. However, there will be yet another party on that day for it is then that the full-scale wedding rehearsal should take place with the bride, groom, both sets of parents and the adult attendants going through the moves of the ceremony under the guidance of the officiating member of clergy. After the rehearsal, all those attending will be entertained by the bride's parents to a celebratory dinner.

On the wedding day itself, the planning has come down to hour-by-hour, minute-by-minute timing. Ceremony minus two hours; the bride begins to dress. Ceremony minus thirty minutes; the organ or orchestra begins to play. Ceremony minus twenty minutes; groom and best man arrive. Ceremony minus five minutes; groom's parents are seated, bride and escort arrive outside. On the hour decided, to the second: entry of the bride.

The ceremony begins. And temporarily the trappings of consumerism, organization, even religion, fall away to reveal once again the fundamental traditions of the wedding as it has always been observed. Various explanations have been put forward for the main features and procedures: the bride is "given away" by her father, perhaps as a survival of the days when she was literally handed over by him upon payment of the bride price; the bride is accompanied by her bridesmaids and the groom by his best man, a reminder possibly of the time when marriage by capture made it necessary for both protagonist to have trusted friends around them; she is likely to be veiled, and this may be to protect her from evil spirits or to symbolize her subjection to her new husband; she will carry flowers, not only ornaments but also magic tokens of her future fruitfulness. Whatever the explanation of these customs, the remarkable fact is that they are rooted in antiquity, superstition and custom, surviving despite the overlays of civilization and religion. The modern American wedding has been criticized for its apparently commercial and ostentatious motivation, but still the strongest element is that which goes back to pre-history.

After the ceremony, the reception—the last party of the whole affair that marks the formal parting of the bride, and groom, from their parents' circle to set up their new home.

Over twenty-five percent of all weddings held in America today are second or third attempts for one or both of the parties concerned. Traditional "white weddings" in a church or synagogue are usually only the custom in the case of first marriages and, despite the changing and more permissive times we are said to live in, seven out of eight of those getting married for the first time choose this form of wedding. Some of the exceptions are very exceptional, however. Weddings have been conducted under water, in the air and on snow and ice. The first underwater wedding was recorded in Puget Sound in 1935, the bridegroom showing all the adventurousness of his seventy-three years. Two German acrobats got married high up on their trapeze, while another couple in Las Vegas soared even higher and had their ceremony circling the city in an airplane. In Vineland, New Jersey, the mayor donned roller skates to marry two keen skaters on the rink, while yet another pair of newlyweds skied away from their ceremony the moment it was concluded. The snow was coming down rather heavily at the time, on top of Squaw Peak in California. Those were quiet ceremonies compared to the recent wedding of a country-and-western star who got married in the world's largest enclosed space, the Astrodome in Houston, Texas. The occasion probably holds the world record for the largest number of guests ever to be assembled in the "church" at a wedding. The service was held at a combined baseball game and concert for which 40,000 seats had been sold. The electronic scoreboards flashed up the names of the bride and groom during the ceremony and afterwards the bride removed a garter from her very shapely leg under the blaze of arclights and the watchful lenses of TV cameras.

OPPOSITE *Mr. and Mrs. (just) Longworth, with President Roosevelt, 1906. A Curtis photograph.*

OPPOSITE *Fact and fiction in romantic American art: the wedding of Pocahontas and John Rolfe, 1614, and the marriage of Hiawatha and Minnehaha.*

THIS PAGE *Two unusual weddings, (left) in 1923, and (below) General Tom Thumb's wedding in 1863.*
BOTTOM *An elegant black wedding, 1929.*

Curiosities and Celebrities
TOP LEFT *New York's first airplane wedding.*
TOP CENTER *A ceremony presided over by Baba*
 Muktananda.
BOTTOM LEFT *A sponsored wedding on TV.*
ABOVE *The wedding of rock star "Sly" Stewart, of Sly*
 and the Family Stone.
LEFT *Mr. and Mrs. David Eisenhower. An hour earlier*
 she had been Julie Nixon.
OVERLEAF *Arlo Guthrie and bride are serenaded by*
 Julie Collins.

Love, money, magic, security, politics: whatever the reasons, they have all contributed to a system which works, and which most of us approve and perpetuate. Violence, payment, bizarre ritual, lavish ceremonial, calculating business transaction: whatever the style, these too have marked the character of an extraordinary human event.

Like monogamy, like the family, marriage seems fundamental to the needs and wishes of most individuals and communities. We have elaborated nature's basic courtship and mating mechanisms to a degree where a wedding is an occasion for joy not only for the bride, groom and their families, but for everybody. As a wedding ceremony marks the creation of a new family unit to link two existing families, so it is at the same time an expression of hope in the future and a reaffirmation of faith in the old values.

Weddings contain color, drama, romance, eccentricity happiness and occasionally the less laudable aspects of human nature. But human they are, tinged too with an element of the supernatural and the wonderful. This irresistible mixture seems likely to guarantee the continued existence of the wedding ceremony for ever.

Picture Credits

The author and publisher wish to thank the following agencies and individuals for giving permission to reprint their photographs.

Black and White Ashmolean Museum, Oxford: 21, 27 (both), 32 (bottom). Associated Press Ltd., London: 251 (bottom). The British Museum, London: 69. Bulloz, Paris: 101. Camera Press, London (Photographer: R. B. Bedi): 156 (bottom), 157 (bottom). Robert Harding Associates, London: 144 (left). Library of Congress, Washington, D.C. (from *The Life of George Washington – The Citizen*: lithograph by Regnier, after Stearns, *c.* 1854): 76. Magnum, New York: 31, 212, 217, 241. The Mansell Collection, London: 12, 20, 32 (top), 41, 52 (both), 55, 58, 60 (top right, bottom), 61 (bottom), 73, 79, 80 (2 insets), 81 (inset), 85 (bottom), 117, 125, 129, 137, 141, 142–3, 146 (bottom), 166, 170–71, 181, 184, 195, 196 (inset), 198 (left), 202, 227. Monkmeyer Press Photo Service, New York (photographer: Mimi Forsyth): 250 (top right). Museum of the City of New York, New York: 247 (from the Byron Collection), 248 (bottom: Currier and Ives lithograph in the Harry T. Peters Collection). National Archives (U.S. Signal Corps.): 229. Kenneth M. Newman, The Old Print Shop, Inc., New York: 249 (top right: Currier and Ives). New York State Historical Association, Cooperstown, N.Y.: 83 (bottom right), 84 (top left). Photo Researchers, Inc., New York (photographer: Katrine Thomas): 198–9. Popperfoto, London: 222–3. Radio Times Hulton Picture Library, London: 62 (bottom right), 77, 78, 80–81 (background picture), 82 (all 3), 83 (bottom right), 91, 99, 123, 127, 144–5, 146 (top), 147, 156 (top), 157 (top), 169, 188, 189, 196–7, 218–19, 236, 248 (top), 249 (top left), 250 (top left, bottom). Rijksmuseum v. Volkskunde Het Nederlands Openluchtmuseum, Arnhem: 96. State Historical Society of Wisconsin: 62 (top left, bottom left), 83 (top: photo by Matthew Witt); 84 (top: photo by Matthew Witt). James van der Zee Institute: 62 (top left), 63, 249 (bottom). Wide World Photos, New York: 251 (top); 252–3.

Color Aldus Books, London: 33. Axel-Poignant, London: 106–7 (both). Barnaby's Picture Library, London: 113 (bottom right). Bulloz, Paris: 40 (top). Cottie Burland: 237 (bottom). Camera Press Ltd., London: 112–13 (left), 114 (top). Curtis Publishing Co.: 240. Daily Telegraph Colour Library: 178–9 (all 3). Granada TV, London: 173. Grandma Moses Properties, Inc., New York: 237 (top). Hannibal, Athens: 35 (bottom left). Robert Harding Associates, London: 105 (inset); 115, 176–7 (main picture). Keystone Press, London: 108 (top left). The Mansell Collection, London: 34–5 (top). Lauros-Giraudon, Paris: 35 (bottom right), 40 (bottom). J. G. Moore: 111. National Gallery, London: 38–9. Photo Meyer, Vienna: 36–7. Picturepoint, London: 108 (bottom left), 113 (top right), 180. Popperfoto, London: 105, 116, 174 (top). Ripley Lantern Slides, Topeka, Kansas: 238–9 (all 4). Scala, Florence: 34 (bottom). *Sunday Times*, London (photo by Don McCullen): 174 (bottom). Syndication International: 108–9 (right); 110.